"Wanderlust"

Is a word that designates a strong desire for or impulse to wander, or, in modern usage, to travel and to explore the World.

This book is dedicated to "Sydney Taylor" and his descendants.

*To Charles J. Elbourne
Hope you have a great
Christmas & a Happy New Year
Marc Cardinal*

Wanderlust

by
Marc Cardinal

**BASED ON THE TRUE-LIFE
JOURNALS OF SYDNEY TAYLOR**

"HUDSON BAY COMPANY" EMPLOYEE
FROM **1902** TO **1952**

AuthorHouse™
1663 Liberty Drive
Bloomington, IN 47403
www.authorhouse.com
Phone: 1-800-839-8640

© 2010 Marc Cardinal. All rights reserved.

No part of this book may be reproduced, stored in a retrieval system, or transmitted by any means without the written permission of the author.

First published by AuthorHouse   2/8/2010

ISBN: 978-1-4490-7907-9 (e)
ISBN: 978-1-4490-7908-6 (sc)

Printed in the United States of America
Bloomington, Indiana

This book is printed on acid-free paper.

Foreword

Few men have had the experience I went through to getting this journal from the Taylor family. I had the urge to re-write this journal in such a way that people of all ages could appreciate the hardships that men in the Hudson Bay Company faced in their daily lives living far from civilization in rough environments. My main idea was to write his journals in such a fashion that information is learned from everything that Sydney Taylor came into contact with.

This story dates back to 1887 when a young lad with a hard childhood decides to run away from home at the age of fifteen. He persevered in his goal of voyaging from England to Canada to start a new life instead of the one that his grandfather had planned for him as a clerk sitting on a stool doing the same thing over and over each day.

I was almost killed one day back in February, 2008 by a bulldozer running over my shiny white 4x4 Silverado half ton truck. It was a miracle that day as the heavy wide treads of the large Caterpillar drove up the hood of my truck and stopped just before it hit the windshield and possibly me. In a later conversation with the driver of the bulldozer, Walter Taylor Jr., I came to know him better and I talked to him about my love of writing and he told me of his grandfather Sydney Taylor who had written his life's story. He told me that it was badly in need of someone who could edit it and make it into a story that could be enjoyed by people. Well over a beer or two later as I thought of it, I knew that I had been saved by a force so powerful that it can only be called the hand of God. I had his help in protecting me that day from being crushed inside a newly rented truck. I told myself that I would write this story.

I have taken many liberties with the family journal to describe what he wrote down from the time he was fifteen until the age of eighty-five. Often it was confusing, with run on sentences, but it was interesting so I wrote it in a fashion that it would appeal to any age. I often think it would make a great school book for children to read, especially for kids going to school in Ontario, Canada. There are probably mistakes in places, events or people but most likely it is my fault and I apologize for such problems if they exist. I'm sure that someone will most likely find them and please feel free to e-mail me so I know of these things. The journal has been greatly researched, mapped and expounded on for the reader.

To be a writer, you have to have passion, creative drive and motivation along with the skills of putting your words onto paper in such a fashion that someone reading it will enjoy the story and get pleasure from spending their precious leisure time relaxing with a good book. I believe I have all of this in me and my goal is to be a successful writer and to write many more varieties of stories.

One thing I can say about taking the chance of publishing your book...follow what you want, what your heart says, follow your dreams. If you think publishing your book will make you happy and make you a better person then do it. I know my wife will understand and support me in my efforts...you know that there's a saying "In every man's success there is a woman behind him."

Also taking a chance and writing a novel that appeals to people is like an investment. You have to invest, produce a capital and this could take months or years before you will know/count your R.O.I (return of investment.). This is my first completed story and I have almost finished a different type of novel to follow close behind. In the writing industry there's always a saying...no pain no gain or high risk high return. How will I know the answer of such things if I am not willing to try? *My goal in writing is to contribute to what has kept people interested in for decades and that is reading.*

This is a picture of me looking for gold in Beardmore, Ontario. Marc Cardinal - Photo 2008

Contents

	Foreword	v
1.	Essex, England - 1887	1
2.	My school Years during 1897 to 1902	7
3.	Running away from Home	20
4.	Voyage to Canada	27
5.	My First Jobs in Canada	34
6.	The Hudson Bay Company	43
7.	My first birch bark canoe trip	49
8.	The White Dog Post	58
9.	The Sturgeon Lake Post	70
10.	The Lac Seul Post	75
11.	Vancouver, British Columbia	85
12.	Jackfish to Longlac	93
13.	The Nipigon Area	100
14.	Sugared Fish and Watered Down Milk	105
15.	Resignation, Prospecting & Duluth, Minnesota - 1908	118

16.	The Call of the Wild Once More	122
17.	Manager of the White Dog Post	133
18.	North to Fort Hope - Eabametoong	144
19.	Spanish Flu, Appendicitis & the HBC 250th Anniversary	158
20.	Longlac, Ontario	163
21.	Oh, how the years go by!	175
22.	Retirement from the Hudson Bay Company	182
23.	Native Population Census & back to the HBC	187
24.	Two pensions and another retirement	195
25.	A visit home to England	203
	Afterword	216
	Biography	218

Researched, edited & illustrated by Marc Cardinal
This story is based on the true-life journals of Sydney Taylor.

Chapter One

Essex, England – 1887

I, Sydney Taylor, was born at Leytonstone which was an area in the north-east section of Greater London and was near the County of Essex in the year 1887.

Life wasn't easy; my mother died when I was four years old leaving me with a sister two years older than myself and a brother five years older. My father was a law officer on some type of ship, always on various voyages and I had no recollection of seeing him. I had no memory of my brother either, as he was gone away to some boarding school and he didn't keep in contact with us.

Life started out quietly for my sister and I and I wondered what life would bring for us.

I have a dim recollection of arriving with my sister in the custody of an aunt at a house in Manningtree which was a small village in the Tendring District of Essex, England. The village adjoined the built-up areas of Lawford, Dedham, Wrabness and Mistley. The collection of parishes and villages together were sometimes referred to as Manningtree.

It was a small town on the border of the River Stour and there we were placed in the custody of two middle aged spinsters, Maria and Amella. We soon took to calling them A&M as it was easiest for us at that time. In fact they were reputed to be very distant relations of our grandmother. The first words I remember them saying was a rebuke to us concerning the behavior that would be expected of us. These were namely strict obedience, no lies and no stealing; these would be punishable by the birch rod.

These two aunts however were good and kind to us as well as being strict. I have no recollection of even seeing let alone feeling the sting of the birch rod. Our custodians had acquired a tannery somewhere in the village. We never got to see it as I suspect they thought it would have an adverse effect on us. In fact we knew nothing about it during the time of our stay with them.

Of more interest to us were the canaries of which they had half a dozen or more in a large cage which was located in the breakfast room. One of these birds was of a brown color and we were told it was a Cape Canary from the Cape of Good Hope in South Africa.

They also kept bees and two hives in their garden. These were of a different pattern to most bee hives being in the form of upright closets of about six feet high with doors at the back. Through the back door of the closet, the empty frames for the honeycombs were inserted and they were removed when they filled up with honey. As I recollect there was glass through which one could observe the bees at work. When the time came to remove the honeycombs, A&M covered their faces with veils and smoked out the bees from their hives by means of a bellow shaped device. This operation of the squeezing and the ejection of the smoke from a nozzle was quite a mystery to us being young children.

Manningtree we figured got its name from the many trees in the area. The village grew around the wool trade and later it had a thriving business in corn, timber and coal with the coming of the railway train way of life.

Later on in life, as I looked back, I learned that Manningtree was known as the center of the activities of Matthew Hopkins. He had appointed himself the Witch Finder General. He claimed to have overheard some local women discussing their meetings with the devil in 1644. His accusations were enough to lead to their execution as witches.

Many of the buildings in the centre of the village had Georgian facades which obscured their earlier origins. This was a type of architecture that was found in most of the English speaking countries and was a common type of architectural style that was widespread between 1720 to around 1840.

The houses were simple and looked like one or two story box buildings; they were deep and had really strict arrangements as to the walls and roof. Usually they had multi-paned windows that were never beside each other but would be spread about five across the front of the house. Mostly they had a chimney on both sides of the building, while the roof would slope at various exact angles with a simple window in the center.

There was a village library, which had originally been built as a public hall for the purposes of the corn exchange business but was now being used as a hall for entertainment. The only other thing I found out as I grew up was that Manningtree had the oldest Methodist church in Essex District and it was located on South Street.

Our house had a garden which was encompassed by a high brick wall of probably six feet, although at the time, being youngsters, it appeared much higher to us. It was only the second time that we were in the garden that we saw strange heads appearing above the wall and making faces at us. They scared the wits out of us appearing so suddenly. We were informed that they were ruffians and it wasn't long until the top of the wall was plastered with cement in which were embedded pieces of broken glass to refrain them from reaching up and hoisting themselves high enough to jump over or possibly climb over.

In due course we were allotted small plots of ground and given a few seeds to plant in a small dark corner of the garden where the sun never penetrated. I forget if the seeds ever came up, but I have a vivid remembrance of the discovery one morning that the rain barrel had been cleaned out. The conglomeration of black muck was deposited all among our plantings. With indignation, we bawled our heads off as we sought out A&M who assured us that it was good for the garden. I at least could not swallow that information and thereafter

I converted my plot into an engineering project which was crowned with success. The pouring water did indeed run downhill. My sister I think stuck to her style of gardening, but with what success I do not remember.

A&M employed a maid, a young buxom lady, who used to sing hymns as she worked, one of which stands out vividly. It was "There is a Happy Land far, far away, where Saints in glory stand high as the day…" My aunts did have a piano which my sister soon learned to play. I was too much of a duffer so my instructions were dropped without much hesitation. I suppose my aunts who did the instructing must have played from time to time, but I have no recollection of it whatsoever. I guess my love of music developed later on in life.

I do however remember quite vividly some gentleman visitor, possibly a relative singing their song "Daisy Daisy give me your answer do" and how he changed the wording from "you'll look sweet upon the seat" to "you'll look sweet with your plates of meat" from which I can but assume that meat was a scarce commodity in our diet. Perhaps he thought it might amuse us as apparently it did.

Once we had a Christmas tree, the only one I can remember when I was seven or eight years old. We had invited a few children from another family. These parents apparently had sent over gifts for their own children. Amongst these was a watch that could be wound up to tell the time. How I yearned for that watch only to find it was not for me. It was not until years later that, by saving my occasional tips of six cents or a shilling I was able to buy a gunmetal watch.

That little mistaken kindness on some parent's part went a long way to spoil that Christmas for me. It would have been better had she given her children their gifts in their own home.

I think our biggest thrills were the occasional passing of the organ grinder and his monkey. The grinder would climb up the buildings with his receptacle to play the music by means of rotating a handle on what was an organ on wheels, commonly known as a hurdy-gurdy. Sometimes we were also entertained by a one man band that played a mixture of instruments all at one time.

Then there was the man with the performing black bear, who'd stop here and there along the street to perform his act. There was also a group known as the German Band, although whether the musicians were actually German or not, I can't say, but I think they were. The band usually consisted of a small group of four or five people and I remember hearing the playing of a trumpet.

The village streets not only afforded our means of transportation but were full of hazards. Mostly they were non-existent except for the occasional runaway horse which would come tearing down the streets with the driver cursing and tugging at the reins. The poor driver had no results until a brave bystander dashed out and grabbed the bridle and brought the horse under control.

Chapter 2

My school Years during 1897 to 1902

When I was ten years old I was sent away to a private boarding school at Ipswich which was located in the eastern region of England. It was a small town in the County of Suffolk which was in the Borough of Ipswich located on the Estuary of the River Orwell. Nearby were located quaint towns such as Felixstowe in Suffolk County and also Harwich and Colchester which were in Essex County.

After one term I was then moved by a family member to another boarding school in Dovencourt which was a small seaside town in Essex. It was near the Port of Harwich at the mouth of the River Stour some ten miles distant from Manningtree. Dovencourt was an older seaside town but the smaller port of Harwich was much better known.

Sometimes I would receive an occasional visit from an aunt who would come by way of train, there being no other means of transportation in those days unless one was fortunate enough to own a horse and carriage.

My recollection of my stay there were of my French lessons of which I have a vivid memory of the pride we took in being able to understand a foreign language. I could understand to some extent the requests to learn the language of French. My teacher said to me "the window should always be kept opened or the door to learning would be closed to us". I could never understand why some inanimate objects were male and some others were female. Also it was hard to know when to use the "le" and "la" in the French language.

Some other recollections are of the cannon balls that were fired at distant targets being towed a few miles out in the ocean. The reverberation of the noise necessitated the opening of our windows to avoid them being broken by the repercussion. I remember some of us standing around a piano and learning to sing that hymn for sailors, "Eternal Father strong to save whose arm has found the pesetons wave...."

I was then sent to another Preparatory School for boys during this year at a little village which I think was called Axdin. A town called Colchester was around two miles away and it was the largest settlement within the Borough of Colchester, in Essex, England. I heard it said that it was the oldest recorded Roman town in the British Isles. Someone told me it was for a time the capital of Roman Britain and was one of the oldest recorded markets. I could see the remains of the old Roman Castle and portions of the broken up Roman road.

Why I was moved to three different schools was a mystery to me as no one sat down and explained it to me.

Prior to leaving to attend this new school my grandfather, with whom I had been staying, instructed me in what I'd have to contend with and not to let the other boys dominate me. He told me to stick up for myself and if need be to resort to the manly art of self-defense. As a result I'd not been at the school for more than a day or two when I decided the time for action had come. I sailed into another lad with fists flying and it was not until I'd administered one black eye and received two in return, that one of the teachers arrived at the scene causing such a hasty dispersal of our audience.

I was pronounced the aggressor by our audience and was confined to the school room during recesses. Then I was ordered to write out a few hundred times *"I must not fight in school"* while at the same time being informed that fighting was strictly forbidden and a repetition of such behavior would result in my being expelled. Apparently my grandfather did not realize that the school was being operated by Quakers who held different views to those he held regarding the manly arts. Many of the Quakers felt that their faith did not fit within the traditional Christian categories of Catholic, Orthodox or Protestant but they believed it was another way of experiencing God.

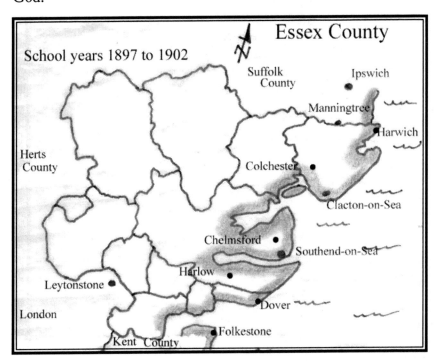

Subsequently I was relieved of my punishment long before I'd completed it and my antagonist became one of my best friends with whom I spent part of my holidays on one occasion.

Around this time I acted on the public stage for entertainment which I enjoyed very much.

It was during this time at the age of twelve that my aunt visited me at school to advise me of the death of my father and she told me then that he had been living at a flat in London all of this time. He had to cut short his three year trip on the SS Norseman to the South Pacific due to a serious heart attack. The ship was engaged in repairing the Trans Pacific telephone cable at this time.

Having only seen my father one or two days while I was growing up, I was apparently not distressed as would normally be the case. It was decided that I should not attend the funeral, and as a result I was accused of lacking in feelings.

I had a cousin attending this school also, but he was in a higher grade and we occupied different dormitories. Our relationship couldn't have made any difference; we could well have been strangers to each other as life goes.

My education was varied and I took many subjects, or rather a smattering of each subject. There was zoology and learning the names and how to recognize such prehistoric animals as Labarynthedonts, Megathurums, Petrodestyls and much more from colored slides. I was also enrolled in courses in Latin, algebra and chemistry which I think did not enter into the school curriculum here until the higher grades.

Directly in front of our school was the Estate of Earl and it had a couple of peacocks which would sometimes pay us a visit and spread their tails in all of their finery.

Amongst the games we played was soccer, which at that time

was nothing as it appears today. I would usually play the part of goaltender. Also, there was cricket and sometimes a game called rounders which was similar to baseball, but played with a cricket bat. Occasionally the boys would play "Fox and Hound", in which two of the best runners would start out with bags of torn up paper and they would scatter it here and there but not very purposely along the fields. They wanted the rest of the boys who were participating and endeavoring to catch up with them to have a path, but they would set numerous blind trails. It was lots of fun on a fine sunny day which was the only time it was played.

Looking out of our dormitory window we could see into the neighbor's yard where we saw two elderly ladies smoking clay pipes. This was the first time we had seen ladies smoking at all and we found it highly amusing. We assumed that they were Irish as we had heard of such things going on in Ireland.

The school property comprised of such things as an outdoor gymnasium as well as a carpenter's shop containing a lathe for those who made carpentry a hobby, but not for those training as prospective carpenters. At the school there was a wood shed where the boys could play but apparently the safety precautions were lax. I remember one boy playing around splitting wood on a block. He placed his hand on the block and was just in time to have the last joint of a finger lopped off. One of the boys had the presence of mind to recover the severed portion just in case it could be sewn back on. I was never really sure what happened afterwards with the detached part of the finger.

Winter came and I observed one of the students throwing snowballs at a teacher who took it good-naturedly. I tried it out myself a few days later, hitting him in the face with a soft one, but alas I discovered that such privileges were not accorded to beginners, or else I caught the teacher in a bad mood. Apart from a good scolding however I don't recollect being punished for it.

The headmaster was a very fine older gentleman in his seventies I think, and although a Quaker he allowed boarding students to attend their own churches. Occasionally though we had to attend a Quaker meeting, where there was no music or hymns and the elders just prayed and sat "until the spirit left them". Indeed it was such a solemn affair and we were awfully bored and strived to stay awake.

On Saturdays we were given our weekly spending money as advised by our parents or guardians, which in my case was a tuppence. This was the equivalent of about eight cents, but which had the purchasing power of about two shillings I would think, enough to buy an orange and a few candies (sweets as we called them). Some of the more fortunate boys had parents who were living and received sixpence or even a shilling which was the equivalent of a quarter. We usually walked to Colchester to spend our allowances, and sometimes whilst there we'd visit the old Roman castle.

Once a week or so we'd be taken to a small hall in Colchester and put through our exercises by a Sergeant, much as I imagine the army cadets are trained. We would exercise with dummy rifles and took other forms of physical training such as the horizontal ladders, club swinging and many more forms of exercise.

Whenever I had holidays from school I'd spend them at my grandfather's house in the Village of Mistley some two miles or so from Manningtree. Most of my time there was spent in his spacious gardens as I was not allowed on the streets, unless I was out on an errand or for a long walk. Amongst my tasks in the garden was the shaking out of earwigs. I would shake them from the inverted flower pots into objects that were set out with sticks two or three feet high and placed here and there along the border for the express purpose of catching these pesky insects which were then tossed into a pail of water.

Then of course there was a little weeding to be done in which I could take part although this was largely left to the hired gardener's attention. There were also two glass houses, one known as the conservatory and the other as a fernery. Smaller garden conservatories were becoming popular around this time and they were used partially as greenhouses for conserving plants and to a degree for recreational use.

The difference that I could see between the two greenhouses was that the fernery was just used for the cultivation of fern-like plants while the conservatory was a rather large greenhouse used for conserving plants. The conservatory was unique in that it had rare plants and often I could spot out some birds and rare animals.

I had heard of but never seen what was called an orangery which was similar to a greenhouse or conservatory but was mainly used for the wintering of citrus trees and to house exotic plants. Around Europe at this time, especially those places in cold climates people were building municipal conservatories to display tropical plants and to hold flower displays. This type of conservatory was popular at the end of the nineteenth century and around when I was living there they were being used to hold social tea parties.

Some of them were so creative and breathtaking in their design; the architecture ranged from typical Victorian glasshouses to modern styles called geodesic domes.

The fernery, which was a specialized garden meant for the cultivation and display of fern plants, was hot and steamy inside and made it uncomfortable for lengthy stays. In the conservatory we had a chameleon which my father had brought home from one of his voyages and it afforded me much interest. The chameleon was also very beneficial in keeping down the insects or flies and it was amazing to see the lightning speed with which its tongue shot out when capturing a fly. It was also interesting to see its color camouflages depending on the color of foliage in which it was hiding.

My grandfather had dogs but these were never allowed in the house but kept chained in the stable yard where their kennels were. I recollect his having a black curly coated retriever, a fox terrier and an old English bob tailed sheep dog. He didn't have them all at the same time; the sheep dog replaced the retriever which had been done away with for some reason. What an ungainly dog the sheep dog was and we called him Mistry Bob. The dogs would often accompany us if we were out for a stroll as was the custom in those days.

We also had pigeons, but these did not have the same attachment to us and were to me just birds among the other many varieties.

Sometimes during the summer holidays we'd go on a picnic in the woods where the primroses, the bluebells and the anemones grew and that my aunt loved to pick. Occasionally, we would go for a boat ride on the River Stour whilst seated in a rowboat which was rowed by one of my grandfather's employees. We would head out to view sites such as the local mills.

Sometimes we made a trip by train to Walton-on-the-Naze and to Clacton-on-Sea.

Walton-on-the Naze was a small town in Essex, England on the North Sea coastline in the Tendring District. It was north of Clacton and south of the Port of Harwich. Close beside this small town was Fricton-on-the-Sea located to the south which was part of the Parish of Fricton and Walton. Clacton-on-Sea was the largest town on the Tendring Peninsula, in Essex, England and had been founded in 1871. Both were very popular English resorts. They both were much favored with their long sandy beaches and at that time not overcrowded but I could see that soon they would become popular recreational locations.

Sundays were very strictly observed and church attendance now or then was not taken for granted and quite often both morning and evening services were attended. Household chores were reduced to a minimum. Even my reading could not be of a frivolous nature; only books or articles that were calculated to improve the mind could be read on a Sunday.

When Christmas rolled along we had no Christmas tree in my grandfather's home, as in those days they were essentially for families with young children. We did however decorate the breakfast, dining room and entrance hall with boughs of holly and mistletoe hung over the drawing room doorway. "Pear Annual", which was a publication put out by the makers of Pear's Soap, always contained three or four large pictures about eighteen inches by twenty-four inches and were very popular for decorative purposes. So we hung these in various places for the duration of the season. I enjoyed the one of a little boy with a long clay pipe from which he was blowing bubbles, presumably of Pear's Soap.

On Christmas Eve, carolers would often come and sing Christmas carols outside, hoping for a small remuneration from the occupants. Sometimes the "waits" which were an assemblage of three or four local musicians would play caroling songs instead. Having no radio, to me they were quite an asset but to some folks they were just a nuisance.

We did not attend any midnight service if indeed there was one which I very much doubted. On Christmas day everyone went to the morning service to heartily participate in the hymns and that seemed to start the day off right. Christmas dinner consisted of turkey and plum pudding. The plum pudding was brought into the room, flaming in brandy, and of course was immediately extinguished. It contained a few small coins and I have no doubt that they were strategically placed to ensure that my sister and I would be lucky enough to get one. The vegetables of course were of minor interest to me as I did not have much interest in such things at that time.

This too was one occasion when we minors were allowed our choice of a glass of Port or even better yet to me was a glass of Champagne. Crackers, the paper ones that are pulled and go off with a snap, containing paper caps or miniature toys, were a must. These were placed beside each plate and pulled apart by the combined efforts of a partner and myself. The paper caps were thereupon donned by recipients and there were much laughter and friendly comments and everybody was in high spirits.

The day after Christmas, Boxing Day, was a holiday during which the household staff which included the servants, the cook and our gardener would be waiting around for their Christmas "box" of a shilling or half crown.

Many individuals, I had learned, inventors, engineers, developers and businessmen had contributed together to produce a radio and it was said that the concepts of a radio and its origins were quite multiple and controversial. The development of the radio spanned several decades, with famous people like Thomas Edison who put his patent in during the year of 1885. I read that the patent was granted as Patent#465971 on December 29, 1891. The radio fascinated me as I learned that Gugliemo Marconi had purchased the Edison wireless telegraphy patent for his own further work in wireless telegraphy. The first radio couldn't transmit sound or speech and was simply called the wireless telegraph. In 1897, Marconi established the first radio station on the Isle of Wight, England. As I heard from some friends Marconi had opened the world's first "wireless" factory in

Hall Street, Chelmsford, England in 1898 and employed around fifty people.

When I was fourteen, or nearly so, I was sent to what was known as a Grammar school which was one of several types of schools in England. It was a sort of advancement from the school that I had attended. It was in that time period a way of getting a secondary education.

Once more I was moved to a new area in the Village of Woodbridge, in Suffolk County which was around fifteen miles from home. Suffolk had a comprehensive education system with fourteen independent schools. It was unusual for the United Kingdom, as Suffolk had a three tier school system in place with Primary Schools having children from five to nine years old, a middle school that continued on from nine to thirteen and then the Upper Schools with older children thirteen to sixteen years old. I don't remember the name of the school; for some reason it eludes me.

I became known as a "fag" as all newcomers were. That meant that one of the boys in the senior grades made use of my services for such things as shining his shoes or maybe running errands for him to the tuck shop or what not. I occupied a dormitory of around ten beds I think.

My recollections of my first year there were few, but I do remember that the place was heated by coal gas. We used to save tin cans, punch a small hole in the bottom over which we'd hold a finger whilst holding the can with the open end over the unlighted gas. We would then place the can on the floor open end down and apply a match to the small hole. The gas would burn down until the quantity of air that replaced the burnt gas was just right to cause an explosion resulting in the tin can flying up maybe six feet or more.

I also remember the tuck shop although with my meager allowance it was more of a source of frustration than anything else.

There was a river not far from school where we used to go swimming and it was not until a boy could swim the half mile or so across the river that he was permitted to go boating. I remember making the attempt but I got into trouble and had to be rescued by one of the graduate swimmers. I didn't have the means to rent a boat anyway so I never repeated the attempt.

During holidays we would often go for walks and sometimes we'd pick up the odd carrot or turnip and eat them on the spot. Wheat when ripe could also be rubbed between the hands, husks blown away and we would eat the grain.

It was during my stay at this school that Queen Victoria died in 1901 and I remember the school attended the church service in remembrance of one who at that time was known as the Good Queen.

During my second term, I was transferred to my new quarters in another residence which was part of the same school but under an assistant headmaster. There I had a study course that I shared with two cousins, brothers of one who had attended my previous school and who was now attending this one. Alas, both of these two roommates of mine were killed in the First World War.

One of my outstanding memories was the arrival of a Siamese Prince as a pupil. As I recollect I was around twelve years of age but I never got around to talking to him as I never seemed to have the chance. It is strange I have forgotten his name; it wasn't that he was of foreign birth, but doubtless that his name was too long.

At this school some of the boys were given garden plots to cultivate. Possibly these were allotted to those not taking any active part in sports. Be that as it may I have no recollection of harvesting any crop and it may well have been that I left school during the summer and never got back to study the results.

My recollection of the "housemaster" was that he was a fine kindly elderly man. It was not so with one of our teachers who was extremely sarcastic and made full use of the cane on us.

With the advent of winter and the wet snow, snowball fights were engaged in between the school boys and the town boys who were not allowed on the grounds. The battles took place at the entry gates and with the snow packed hard, sometimes a stone would lodge itself in the centre and someone could have really gotten hurt. However, I have no recollection of any serious wounds, such as would have happened if someone had gotten hit in the eyes.

Chapter 3

Running away from Home

Alas, when exam time came around, I failed to pass and as a result my grandfather took me out of school. He then gave me a job as a junior clerk in a fire insurance office. Here I used to write out insurance policies for large sums per month; sometimes they were roughly the equivalent of six dollars.

I in turn had to hand over my earnings to my grandfather who in turn allowed me a shilling a week for spending money. Fair enough no doubt in view of the fact that he was paying for my lodging and clothing. I had no need for money except to buy candy and I was too young to smoke.

I was boarding with a guy named Proper who owned a tannery which in this case was at the rear of the property. The owner's Christian name was Latimer and he had a brother living next door by the name of Reilley. They were named after two Christian martyrs who were burnt at the stake. I was now working in the historical Town of Bury St Edmunds, the site of an old Norman Tower as well as the Abbey Tower and an inn that was mentioned in Charles Dickens's novels.

Bury St Edmund was a very historic market town in the County of Suffolk, England and I was fascinated by the history of the place each time I walked by the ruined Abbey near the town center. It was supposed to have been the Villa Faustina of the Romans and was one of the royal towns of the Saxons. Sigebert, the King of East Angles had founded a monastery in this location back in 633, and which in turn became the burial place of King Edmund, who was slain by the Danes in 869. By the year 925 the reputed miracles performed at the shrine spread and a town grew around the Bury St Edmund Abbey. The site became known as a site for pilgrimages and by 925 the town's name was changed to St Edmund Bury. Sometimes it is written Bury St Edmund or Bury Saint Edmund on the maps of the area.

On Sundays I'd attend services at sundry village churches which meant that I was attending various and diverse styles of churches. They were all within a few miles, and I must admit that the walks to and from these various villages afforded me as much pleasure as the service. If the service was too long or of little interest I suppose the walks gave me more pleasure.

Walks through the Abbey gardens were also a source of pleasure and on one occasion I saw a very shabby old man puttering around amongst the plants and I assumed that he was the gardener but I subsequently found out that he was a Lord. I'm not sure what this title meant but I had heard it could denote a prince or a feudal superior but then again it could have meant Lord Mayor. To me it was just a title used to denote a superior holder or some sort of title. I did tend to find it amusing that this Lord who was working the garden, old and shabby, was actually the owner of the property.

I think it was here that I became cognizant of the funny papers, which were then known as comics. Anyways I remember the funny papers a little but it was Alexander "Ally" Sloper that stuck out in my mind. This was one of the earliest fictional comic strip characters. He was red-nosed and blustery, definitely a lazy schemer who was found sloping through the alleys to avoid his landlord and other creditors. I doubt if my meager salary would permit me buying any comics that would have been regarded as trash.

Occasionally I was able to rent a bike and travel around the countryside, but I never owned one.

Alas, the office work was far from my liking and I'd always dreamed of being a sailor. This was far from my grandfather's way of thinking, failing that I could think of nothing else but being stuck on a stool in an office all day.

I began to formulate plans for running away; I expect most kids do. I took little thought as to how I could find work and accommodations. The idea of stealing my earnings was repugnant to me, but then I consoled myself with the thought that I'd actually be saving my grandfather money for my upkeep.

I don't think on looking back that I could have given any serious thought as to how I'd obtain employment.

Whatever the reason I can't recall, but presumably it was in my own mind to make sure that I went first across the English Channel from Folkestone. This was the principal town in the Shepway District of Kent, England. Folkestone was in the County of Kent which was below Essex County so I'd be traveling through three counties to get to my destination. I'd start out in the middle of Suffolk County at Bury St. Edmund, head to London, travel through Essex County and end up at the south-east section of the County of Kent which was on the coast of the English Channel separating England and France.

The town had originally developed through fishing and I had heard that it lay in a stream valley in the cliffs of the area.

Wanderlust

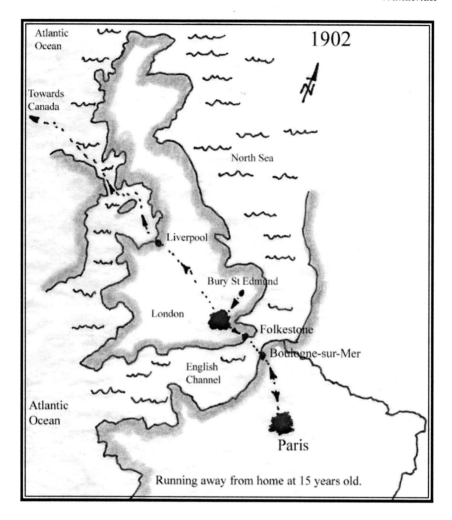

Running away from home at 15 years old.

One evening I procured a length of string strong enough to hold a Gladstone bag, which was a hinged luggage brown leather traveling bag. This luggage bag was all that I had to take; it was later called a portmanteau and was new to the times having a rigid frame which could be separated into two equal sections. It was made of stiff leather and was belted with lanyards. I used the lanyards sometimes around the neck or on my wrist to carry my Gladstone bag. I wasn't going to take any chance of losing it and in this way it was visible at all times.

I had purchased it because it was given its name after our popular Prime Minister of the United Kingdom who was noted for the amount of traveling that he did. I figured that it would probably be best for the travels that I had planned.

I went to my room and put on my Sunday best, packed my bag and lowered it from my bedroom window into the backyard. I then came down, stuck my head in the parlor door and told the lady of the house that I was attending a meeting in town. I then went into the backyard and picked up my bag where I walked down to the Station and boarded a train to the Liverpool Street Station in London. After that I walked all the way to the Cannon Street Station.

That evening after finding a room to stay at overnight I waited for the morning train, sitting nervously on my bed. I was starting to feel some trepidation about what I had set myself up to do. Again while riding on the train to Folkestone I felt the same, but decided I couldn't go back and if I did I wouldn't be able to go through with it another time.

How well I remember my arrival at Folkestone where it was blowing a regular gale and it was here that I first saw the English Channel. This was an arm of the Atlantic Ocean that separated England from Northern France and led into the North Sea which eventually joined the Atlantic Ocean. It varied in width from somewhere around one hundred miles at its widest to about only twenty miles in the Straight of Dover. It was well known to be the smallest of the shallow seas around the continental shelf of Europe.

However the English Channel was noted for its rough seas. And it wasn't long before I felt some qualms in embarking on the small passenger boat. It wasn't long after we left before I became seasick for the first time; however the trip was short, possibly two or three hours long.

When I arrived at Boulogne-sur-Mer on the northern tip of France which was a commune in the north-eastern part of the country, I decided a cup of tea might help. I dropped into the first restaurant that presented itself and was immediately joined by a fellow passenger, who had been sitting across the table from me. When he learned that Boulogne-sur-Mer, France was as far as I planned to go, he suggested that I must really see Paris which was only a short distance away.

He suggested that he would show me some of the sights and so I agreed. Arriving at Gare Saint-Lazare Station in Paris which was one of the six large train Stations of Paris and the second busiest, we each found rooms in a small hotel by the name of Hotel Amsterdam. It was here that we secured separate rooms and that was the last that I saw of him.

The next morning when I came down and inquired at the desk I was told that he had booked out and left. He was a commercial traveler and had seemed a nice enough chap so maybe a change in his schedule had necessitated his taking an early train out.

So there I was, only fifteen years old and in a foreign city.

Fortunately the little French I had learned in school stood me in good stead as when my friend ran out and payment for my accommodations was demanded. I was able to say "Je n'ai pas d'argent mais quand mon ami reviendra, il m'en prêtera." This meant I hope, that "I have no money but when my friend returns he'll lend me some".

Anyways that got me off the hook for a few days until he returned. I took advantage of the time and roamed around the city walking towards the Eiffel Tower. This was an iron tower built on the Champs de Mars beside the Seine River in Paris. The Champ de Mars was a large green space located in Paris and had the Eiffel Tower to the north-west and the Ecole Militaire to the south-east.

The area was named after Campus Martius of Rome and the name Champ de Mars meant the "Field of Mars" after Mars, the God of War.

This tower had become a global symbol of France and one of the most recognizable structures in the world. I looked at the bronze sign next to the stairway leading upwards; it had been named after its designer Gustave Eiffel from 1887 the year I was born until it was completely constructed in 1889. I was a little frustrated as it being winter I was only able to go halfway up which was a great disappointment to me.

Of course I found the city magnificent especially the Avenue des Champs-Élysées. This was the most prestigious Avenue in Paris, France. It was lined with cinemas, cafés and luxury specialty shops. The Avenue des Champs-Élysées was one of the most famous streets in the world and I heard someone talking about the astronomical prices for rent and that it was the most expensive strip of real estate in Europe.

One day in my wanderings which were quite extreme, I lost my way, stopping people here and there, but somehow I always managed to find my way back.

Money was an issue and I couldn't stay long in France so I decided in my mind that Canada was the place that I wanted to move to and make my home. As I returned back across the English Channel I knew I had to make a final visit to my grandfather and it was a matter of considerable dread to me as he was a very stern and strict man.

My fears however were unfounded as I was not found lying on the carpet so to speak. I just listened to his puny advise and suggestions and he hoped that in a matter of a very few years I'd have a hundred acres and a farm of my own.

Chapter 4

Voyage to Canada

IN DUE COURSE, I entrained during the night for Liverpool which was a city and Metropolitan Borough of Merseyside, England along the eastern side of a body of water called the Mersey Estuary.

A man seated next to me on the train talked constantly about his knowledge of the history of the area. At first I found myself just wanting privacy but then I grew interested and started asking him questions. The man tugged at his high tight collar tied tightly with a beige colored tie that was the style of the day. He rubbed his hands through his thick brown hair and starting describing the City of Liverpool. His mannerism took me to believe that he may have been or was presently a professor at one of the more prestigious schools in the area.

I soon found out that Liverpool, England was founded as a Borough in 1207 and was granted City status in 1880. Historically, he noted, moving his spectacles into a more comfortable position, the inhabitants of Liverpool were commonly referred to as Liverpudlians but were also known as "Scoucers". This was in reference to the local dish known as Scouce, which was a new type of stew of which I hadn't heard of.

I started to laugh thinking of the name Scouce as a meal but then I thought to myself that the English food though tasteless in my opinion did come up with the most original of names and I started passing on some names to my new friend while he wrote them down and added ones that he thought amusing. The best ones that we listed were Bangers and Mash, Toad in the Hole, Spotted Dick, Faggot and Peas, Jellied Eels, Bubbles and Squeak, and now I added Scouce as a new one next to Ploughman's Lunch.

With this topic of food, I soon started wondering what they ate in Canada as I had never thought to look into the subject.

I thanked him for the information as I left the train, passing through the crowds and seeing all around me a wide and diverse population of people, cultures and religions.

As quickly as I could I ran up the plank with its huge knotted ropes on each side which were used to steady oneself as one walked upwards onto the ship. I could see that the ship was about ready to sail. My last glimpse of England at that time was of the three graces of Liverpool's waterfront which I was told were the Royal Liver Building, the Canard Building and the Port of Liverpool Building. Away in the distance I could see the elegant Anglican Cathedral as the ship left the English shoreline.

I had embarked on the S.S. Parisian one of the "Allan Line of Royal Mail Steamers" that was founded in 1854 as the "Montreal Ocean" Steamship. It had later been re-named as the Allan Line after one of its founders, Hugh Allan. In 1891 the company took over the State Line and many of those ships that were in service at that time. The S.S. Parisian was setting sail for what was to me a new world, and soon Liverpool was left in the far distance as the high crests of the waves crashed against the ship as it made its way to Québec City in the Province of Québec and then onward to Toronto in the Province of Ontario, Canada.

Interestingly enough, I noted from people conversing with one another that these were both the capital cities of each of these provinces. I was glad that I would get a chance to see each of them and observe the differences between them, although in my mind I planned to go further than these two large cities since I was hoping to see some of the places I had read about in articles about northern Ontario.

We hadn't been aboard long before we were on our way across that rough piece of water known as the Irish Sea which separates the islands of Ireland and Great Britain. We were heading south by St. George's Channel. The Captain was probably keeping an eye out in the dark for the Island of Anglesey, which was the largest island in the Irish sea followed by the Isle of Man.

It was not however until we went down to dinner and I was all set to enjoy what appeared to be a truly sumptuous meal that the sea sickness struck me suddenly. I made a hurried departure after my first mouthful. After rushing for the deck and leaning over the rail, I heaved up from my stomach, giving the fish below some partially digested food.

I was told that looking at the sea and the rising and falling horizon as the ship rolled in the heavy waves was the worst thing to do. I managed to stagger over to a sheltered spot near the bow, and there I stayed until some sailor grabbed hold of me saying that no passengers were to remain on deck. I returned to my berth, which was an upper one in a three bed compartment and there I remained for a week until we entered the St. Lawrence River.

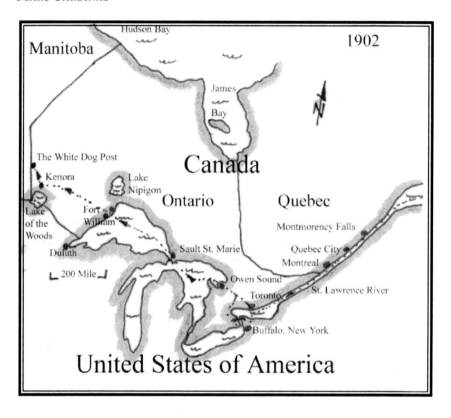

I do distinctly remember the ship pushing through some pans of broken ice. I also recall seeing icebergs some miles away. This month of May was a bad season for ice floes and icebergs borne south on the Labrador Current. This current of water flowed south along the coast of Labrador and passed around Newfoundland, continuing south along the east coast of Nova Scotia. Here it met up with the warmer Gulf current at the Grand Banks through which we were passing. The combination of the two currents produced heavy fogs and was one of the richest fishing grounds in the world.

I also remember seeing some whales spouting alongside of a school of flying fish.

The trip up the St. Lawrence was grand and the Montmorency Falls was one point of interest that I remember being pointed out to me. The Montmorency Falls was a large waterfall in Québec, Canada and they were located near Québec City. They were the highest in the province. A passenger told me that they were measured to be one hundred feet higher than Niagara Falls located in the next province which I now knew was Ontario.

I was fascinated by the waterfall and decided that in the future I must see what he called Niagara Falls.

Shortly before we arrived in the Province of Québec, someone stated that we were to have some of that wonderful maple syrup at our next meal. I looked forward to this treat as I had heard of it in England where it was often eaten with waffles, pancakes and French toast. My grandfather never allowed the use of sweets in the house so I expected much from this sweetener made from the sap of maple trees.

I must confess it was not nearly up to my expectations. This was probably no doubt due to having an exaggerated idea of what to expect.

I forget when the pilot first came aboard to steer us through the St. Lawrence River to our destination, the first for some passengers being the City of Québec, where we would continue on to Montréal. We were given an hour or more to get a brief view of Québec City. I got to see Château Frontenac which was a grand hotel and had been designed by Bruce Price. It had opened in 1893 and was one of a series of Château style hotels built for the Canadian Pacific Railway. The railway owners were seeking to encourage luxury tourism and they desired to bring wealthy travelers to their trains.

The hotel was named in honor of Louis de Buade, Count of Frontenac, who was Governor of the Colony of New France from 1672 to roughly 1698. The Château was built not too far from the historic Citadel, whose construction Frontenac had begun at the end of the 17th century.

Although several of Québec City's buildings stood taller, the Château Frontenac was perched atop a tall cape overlooking the mighty St. Lawrence River. It thus gave a spectacular view for several miles. It was also built near the Plains of Abraham which I had studied while in school. The plains were named after Abraham Martin, who was called "the Scot" who had lived during the years of 1859 to 1664. Abraham had been a fisherman and a river pilot and always brought his animals to graze on the land which he owned.

I remember that the first references to the current area's name were from military documents which were penned by Chevalier de Levis and the Marquis de Montcalm who referred to it as the "Heights of Abraham". Even the journals of the British soldiers that described the Battle of the Plains of Abraham called it the "Heights of Abraham" but it was at this time known as the "Plains of Abraham".

I stood on the Plains of Abraham next to a Martello Tower, which was a small defensive fort standing around forty feet high, containing within it two floors for a garrison of one officer and somewhere around fifteen to twenty men. I leaned on the sturdy round structure made of thick walls of solid masonry making them resistant to cannon fire, while their height made them an ideal platform for a single heavy artillery cannon. This artillery piece was mounted on the flat roof, was able to traverse a three hundred and sixty degree arc and could easily be aimed at approaching enemy ships.

Dreamily, I thought of my teacher back home who had taught us about the war that had happened in Canada; if only my teacher could see this beautiful area. He had taught me the history of this exact spot and how on September 13, 1759, this area was the scene of the Battle of the Plains of Abraham during the French and English Wars in which the British Army under James Wolfe had climbed the steep cliff under the city in darkness. They then surprised and defeated the French.

Both Wolfe and the French commander Montcalm died of their wounds but the battle left control of Québec City to the British who then went on to take control of Canada the following year with the surrender of Montréal.

As I stared around I remembered the ship and the time and I quickly ran down the cobbled streets and was out of breath when I arrived at the S.S. Parisian. I struggled to catch my breath as I hurried up the plank of the ship as it was lifted behind me.

Chapter 5

My First Jobs in Canada

I ARRIVED IN Toronto, Ontario, Canada in 1902 and the first thing that I thought of was, "Here I am in a foreign country, fifteen years old, with hardly any money and what I do have in my pocket is in British currency".

I knew that I would have to find a job as soon as possible.

I hiked up the hill taking in the sights and my first point of interest was the burnt out ruins nearby. They ran for blocks just across what appeared to be a station of some type. It was the aftermath of a fairly recent fire I believe. My destination was the Scarborough Heights, but having no knowledge of how to get there I asked a policeman on the corner of Yonge and Queen Street where I could catch a train to Scarborough.

"Train", he said, "you mean streetcar". I was instructed to take a Danforth Avenue car, get off at some forgotten building, a Chapel, I think it was, and walk from there. I looked at the rail-borne vehicle, which was of a lighter weight and construction than a train, and, from the people going in, it appeared to be designed for transporting people throughout Toronto, or wherever there were train tracks built into the streets.

I looked at the policeman confused and said that it looked like a train to me. He was a large man with a huge belly which stretched his policeman's outfit to the limits and he shook as he laughed. He told me that there were many names for this means of transportation. They were called tram, tramcar, trolley, trolley car or streetcar as he called it. He told me that some people even called it trolleybus or cable car but no one ever called it a train. He told me that a trolleybus was one that had rubber tires and did not conduct electricity so the neutral current couldn't pass directly to the ground whereas an electric tram made use of its steel wheels to take the current to the ground via the tramway rail.

Seeing my confused face, he laughed again and shoved me onto the correct streetcar heading towards where I wanted to go which was the Danforth Avenue streetcar. Inside was a plaque which read that the road which was named after the contractor Asa Danforth who built Queen Street and Kingston Road.

In Scarborough, Danforth Road is part of the original road that connects Danforth Avenue with McCowan Road. I noted that it was possible, therefore, to stand at the intersection of "Danforth Avenue and Danforth Road". Probably the locals were careful to note whether it was the Avenue or Road that was being referred to.

The route continued around Highland Creek along a road called the Painted Post Drive towards the end of Danforth Avenue where I started to walk to my destination which was the Scarborough Heights. I looked at the ad I had taken down from one of the telephone posts as I walked along towards what appeared to be a job working on a local farm.

I judged it entailed a walk of about a mile down a country road, so I cut down a willow tree which I stuck through the handle of my bag carrying it on my shoulder. My destination was a farm, the location of which I had to ascertain by inquiring along the route.

Just how far this was from the Scarborough Bluffs I don't know but I imagined it must have been quite close. I would have liked to have seen them as a fellow passenger had commented on this unique waterfront escarpment which reached two hundred feet high and fifty miles in length.

At the farm there were two other hired men whose bedroom I shared, one of whom I remember commenting on the fact that I had a straight razor but nothing on my face to shave. This I had purchased en route to the streetcar as a little bit of hopeful foresight I expect.

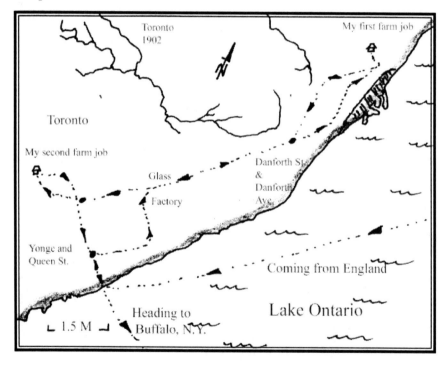

The next morning I was taken to the field and instructed in the odorous art of spreading the piles of manure that had been hauled from the stables and left in piles here and there. I must say I was amazed to learn that even such a task required a knack in the twisting of the four pronged fork to insure an even distribution. Also I felt some umbrage at being given so humiliating a task.

I decided that it must be my nationality which was the reason, the farmer being Scotch or at any rate bearing a Scotch name. My next anger was directed towards one of the helpers that evening when he jokingly remarked the English and Irish didn't amount to anything better than that darn old Dutch farmer.

I forget how many days I stayed there but it must have been less than a week for when Sunday came my fellow workers suggested that I accompany them to a church service in some Chapel, the denomination of which escapes me. It was probably an Anglican church but never having attended one before it did not appeal to me. I left before they did or else I lost them in the congregation en route out as I felt it was time to leave and I headed back to Toronto.

The next day I started visiting employment offices and in the course of a day or two I had secured work in a stained glass window factory on Church Street.

Having no experience in such work I forget just what the work entailed other than sorting over piles of stained glass, and in any case it was of short duration, for just a day or so. I then returned to the unemployment office where I was hired by another farmer for the large sum of ten dollars per month along with room and board.

The fact that I was inexperienced and not very strong I soon found out when I was expected to shoulder two bushel bags of wheat weighing one hundred and twenty pounds each. Once I had been shown the knack, though, I did not find it too strenuous, having only to handle the bushel containers from time to time.

I had never learned how to plough which in those days was all done by horses and, after endeavoring to teach me how, the farmer gave up.

My new duties now entailed getting up very early at five a.m. and milking a number of cows before breakfast and fielding the livestock. During the rest of the day I was engaged in such tasks as churning the butter and hauling rocks on the stone boat from the field to build up the stone fences. A stone boat was a device much like a flat-bottom boat that I used to pull the heavy objects which in this case were stones and weighed a lot. I often swore at it while I was pulling obnoxious weeds from the fence corners.

During the day I did hay work, raking the hay from the fields into small racks and later forking them onto the hay wagon. There was always lots to do but the dirtiest job was standing on a straw stack and stacking the straw as the conveyor belt or sometimes a blower would smother me with dust and fine particles and what looked like vegetation, thistles and much more.

The big reward working at harvest time was the meals that the farmers' wives dished out and there were piles of food that was much appreciated.

The fall came and I was informed that, there being little to do in October, my wages would be reduced to three dollars per month during the fall and winter months. I indignantly refused to accept this so once again I set out for faraway fields.

I had decided that I simply must see Niagara Falls whence after spending the day there I proceeded to Buffalo, New York in the United States as my meager funds were nearly gone.

I must tell you of one episode that happened to me and that was my taking on a job one night shoveling snow after a heavy storm. This I recollect was down in some railway yards where we had to shovel the heavy wet snow and ice into railroad cars.

I didn't know how many of us there were, but most were Italians and Austrians, I think. Anyways by the time we quit in the early hours of the morning I was so tired, more than I think I'd ever been. This was probably caused mainly from the lack of sufficient food for the past few days.

Passing a small lunch counter on the way back to my quarters, I dropped in and asked the lady for a glass of water. She brought me a steaming cup of cocoa and I soon explained to her that I had no money, but she said it was alright, it didn't matter. It was that one act of kindness I've never forgotten; she must have known that I was all done in.

I took on a job as a messenger boy for a telegraph office, the name of which escapes me. In the course of my duties delivering telegrams, some well meaning gentleman gave me a membership ticket to the YMCA, but I was disappointed to find that this did not cover any of the many facilities outside of admission to the library and the reading room.

It did however eventually provide me with the means of obtaining employment at Railroad YMCA in Fort Erie, Ontario, which was a small town on the Niagara River in the Niagara Region and was just across the River from Buffalo, New York in the United States.

This organization was founded in 1844 in London, England by George Williams. It had been originally intended to put Christian values into practice, but things always change.

Young men who came to London looking for work often found themselves living in squalid and unsafe conditions. The Young Men's Christian Association was dedicated to replacing life on the streets with prayer and bible study. The idea was started by the Evangelist and was unusual in that it crossed the rigid lines that separated all the different churches and social classes in England in those days.

This openness and tolerance were traits accorded to the YMCA. All men, women and children, regardless of race, religion, or nationality were treated equally. The YMCA's goal of meeting the social needs in the community was an important right from the beginning and it soon had spilled over to Canada and the U.S.A.

The Railroad YMCA, which was located on Eerie Street, offered me the truly magnificent salary of twenty-five dollars per month along with meals.

At my job at the Railroad YMCA, I was on night shift as a call boy, and amongst some janitorial duties I had to call certain railroad employees for their trains. Most of these people were lodged on the premises, but sometimes we had to phone them at their house and provide a wake-up call for them.

Alas! I really don't think the importance of these calls had been sufficiently impressed upon me, but in any case I once omitted to call an engineer who was due to take one of the passenger trains of the New York Central. Well our YMCA Secretary received a most irate call and the caller requested to talk to me personally. The secretary was extremely worked up and refused to let me on the phone; he was a fine man and I was glad of that.

It was not long after that however that I was transferred to a Railroad YMCA in Bridgeburg, Ontario. This is just near Fort Erie and in fact probably part of that town now. The Town of Fort Erie served places such as Bridgeburg, Ridgeway, Stevensville and Crystal Beach.

Well, I got off to a bad start there when I engaged in fisticuffs with some lad whom I assume was occupied in the same type of work I'd been doing in Buffalo, New York, in the United States. I don't recall what the provocation was, but I do remember that his popularity with the railroad men tended to ostracize me for some days thereafter.

I was then appointed as a night clerk and had a lounge where I could nap until some incoming railroad men would knock on the desk or ring the bell. I then had to ascertain what they wanted to eat and in that case it was usually a choice of bacon and eggs, hamburgers, hotdogs, or sometimes a steak.

The art of cooking these was quickly acquired as well as heating up canned soup and vegetables and making whatever they wanted in the way of beverages. I would also assign them to whatever room might be available. Some nights I was only called upon to perform these duties two or three times and even less and as a result, could secure all my necessary sleep during the night and have practically all of the day to myself.

My favorite event was climbing up the freight trains and running along the tops of the slow moving trains, knowing just how far it was safe to ride before hopping off.

After spending half of the winter and early spring here, the "wanderlust" took hold of me once more and I tendered in my resignation. I remember my boss, the secretary on day duty who was a Baptist and who would not allow me to smoke on the premises, commenting on the fact that now I could smoke all I wanted.

Chapter 6

The Hudson Bay Company

My next venture was to be the Town of Fort William, which was located in Northern Ontario on the Kaministiquia River at the entrance of huge Lake Superior. The Kaministiquia River emptied into western Lake Superior with two large islands McKellar and Mission at its mouth. The river was a Native Ojibwe word meaning river with islands. So in fact it formed a delta with three branches or outlets.

The south-western branch was known as the Mission River, the central branch, the McKellar River, and the northern most one as the Kaministiquia River.

To the north of the two towns was a small curved bay called Thunder Bay; it was located just north of the entrance of the North Current River which went into Boulevard Lake, from there entering Lake Superior. From Thunder Bay could be seen a huge rock formation called the Sleeping Giant which had the form of a large man lying on his back and at the tip of this area was a steep slope which was called Thunder Cape.

The area got its name from the 18th century French maps as "Baie du Tonnerre" which of course meant Thunder Bay in English and it remained as the name of the area.

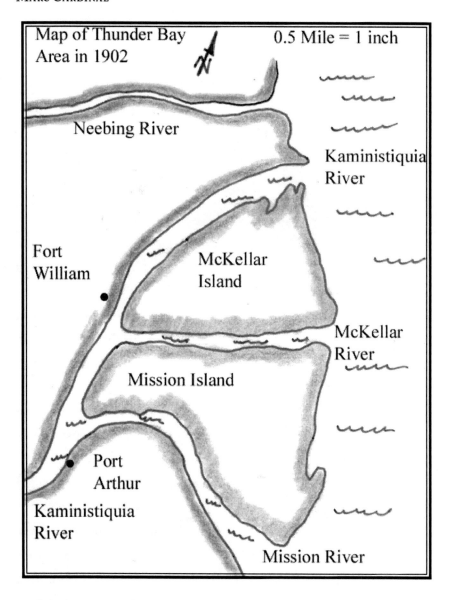

Thunder Bay, the name attracted me, the sound of it fascinated me for some reason as I had nothing in sight to attract me there. In due course I embarked from Owen Sound on the ship S.S. Alberta and arrived in Fort William with enough cash to keep me going for a few days.

Fort William was started in 1679 by Daniel Greysolon, Sieur

du Lhut who established it as a trading post near the mouth of the Kaministiquia River.

The Post was named Fort William in 1807 after William McGillivray, Chief Director of the North West Company from 1804 to 1821. After the union of the North West Company with the Hudson Bay Company in 1821, the Fort lost its reason for being there and became a minor part of the Hudson Bay Company.

It was in the month of August that I was walking down the streets of Fort William looking for a job. I thought to myself that, if I had come to Canada to make my fortune well, this was the time since the ten dollars or so that I had arrived with was all but gone. I found myself without a job, no friends, no money and a long way from home. It didn't really bother me a great deal as I was young, healthy and ready and willing to take on any honest job that I could pick up. As I headed down Simpson Street I was stopped by what looked like a laborer but turned out to be a prospector who asked me for directions. I told him I didn't know the area well and was a stranger in town looking for work.

This man was forever to change my life.

"Why don't you go and see the District Manager at the Hudson Bay Company store? His office is just above the store and he might give you a job at one of the fur trading posts." he suggested. He told me to go upstairs and enquire for a Mr. Trimayne who was the District Manager of the fur trading posts in the area.

Well this really sounded fantastic to me, what did I know about Indians or furs? Giving it some thought I decided to take his suggestion anyway and sure enough Mr. Trimayne, after giving me a try in his office extending and adding inventory sheets, hired me as a clerk assistant at a place called "White Dog" which was a small Indian settlement which was around forty-six miles north of a town called Kenora on the Winnipeg River.

Mr. Trimayne started telling me about the Hudson Bay Company. It was the oldest commercial corporation in North America and probably the world and it was incorporated by the British Royal Charter in 1670 as "The Governor And Company of Adventurers" of England trading into the Hudson Bay Company. It was the largest landowner in the world, with Rupert's Land being part of North America. Its longtime headquarters was at York Factory on Hudson Bay, which he explained to me was a huge body of water at the north part of Canada; it controlled the fur trade throughout much of British-controlled North America. This went on for several centuries, and they undertook the early exploration of Canada and the United States.

Whilst I was at Fort William in the Hudson Bay Company office, I had looked over a faded map on the office wall showing the neighboring towns of Port Arthur and Fort William and the Hudson Bay Company posts located in northern Ontario. With a piece of paper given to me and the use of a pencil I sketched out the area where I'd be working. As an after- thought I added the names of all the other Hudson Bay Company posts in northern Ontario in case I was eventually sent to another.

Along the side of the map was a description that said that Fort William occupied a flat section of land that my boss called alluvial land along the Kaministiquia River. Port Arthur on the other hand had rougher land and he stated this area was more typical of the Canadian Shield which was comprised of gently sloping hills and very thin soil which lay on top of the bedrock with many bare outcrops of rock.

Wanderlust

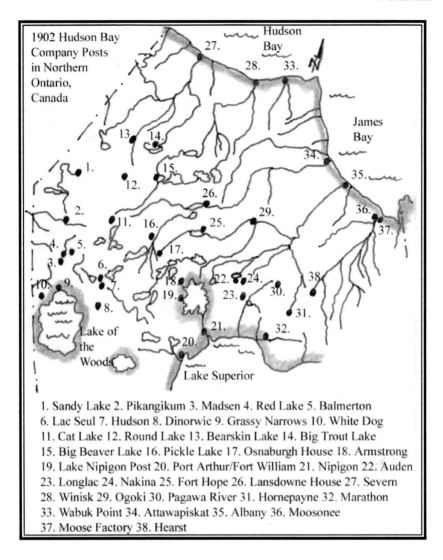

1902 Hudson Bay Company Posts in Northern Ontario, Canada

1. Sandy Lake 2. Pikangikum 3. Madsen 4. Red Lake 5. Balmerton 6. Lac Seul 7. Hudson 8. Dinorwic 9. Grassy Narrows 10. White Dog 11. Cat Lake 12. Round Lake 13. Bearskin Lake 14. Big Trout Lake 15. Big Beaver Lake 16. Pickle Lake 17. Osnaburgh House 18. Armstrong 19. Lake Nipigon Post 20. Port Arthur/Fort William 21. Nipigon 22. Auden 23. Longlac 24. Nakina 25. Fort Hope 26. Lansdowne House 27. Severn 28. Winisk 29. Ogoki 30. Pagawa River 31. Hornepayne 32. Marathon 33. Wabuk Point 34. Attawapiskat 35. Albany 36. Moosonee 37. Moose Factory 38. Hearst

I was however informed that the Company did not pay big wages and I was asked what was the least that I would accept. Tobacco and clothing would be all that I would have to buy, so I said ten dollars a month. Seeing that I had no knowledge of the work Mr. Trimayne said, "Oh, I think we can do a little better than that, how about fifteen dollars instead?" So to me that was a good start and I signed a contract for one year only. This was shorter than usual. Most of the clerks hired in Scotland or the Bikney Islands who worked for the Hudson Bay Company had to enlist for up to three years.

Chapter 7

My first birch bark canoe trip

I WAS THEN given my transportation to Kenora, Ontario and a letter to the Post Manager. It asked him to secure accommodations for me at one of the local hotels until such time as there was an opportunity for me to embark for the White Dog Post.

Kenora, Ontario, which was originally named Rat Portage, was a small city situated on a large body of water known as the Lake of the Woods in north-western Ontario and was close to the Manitoba border. I heard that it was about one hundred miles east of Winnipeg, Manitoba.

It was in 1836 that the Hudson's Bay Company established a post on Old Fort Island, and then in 1861, the Company opened a post on the mainland which was where I was headed and was now the current location of Kenora. A fellow passenger told me that it was a long train ride and I would be heading through the rough terrain of north-western Ontario.

I asked him for some information about where I was going and about the history of the area. He told me that, in 1878, the Company surveyed lots for permanent settlement of Rat Portage, and that name was kept until 1905, when it was renamed Kenora. They made up the name Kenora by combining the first two letters of Keewatin and Norman, which were two nearby settlements, to Rat Portage. As I thought of it I realized that this was really something: Ke-No-Ra, Kenora, what a neat way to name a place!

Both gold and the railway were important in the community's early history. Gold was first discovered in 1850 and by 1893 it had twenty operating mines within what was then Rat Portage. We had to travel along the Canadian Pacific Railway, there being no other way to get there except going through the rocky land and forest by canoe and portages.

Rat Portage or Kenora, whatever the people wanted to call it, was a small town of ill repute with storied brothels collected along the early Canadian Pacific Railway. "Marathon Realty" had gathered large tracts of land which were allocated to them for the purpose of gathering and controlling lands along the railway for commercial and development purposes. I heard later on that people had excavated the garbage dumps adjacent to the brothels and found opium bottles, champagne bottles and pickle jars.

Walking into one of the stores to purchase a few supplies of medicine in case I needed it up in the bush, I found suppliers of patent medicines from Johnson's Pharmacy and at that time they had stuff like Lydia Pinkam's Vegetable Compound, Kickapoo Indian Oil, Dr. Thomas Electric Oil and lots more. Feeling that these were ridiculous I walked back out of the store and saved myself some money.

After staying a night at the recommended hotel I toured the area and found that it was not to my liking and was glad to get on the move as my wanderlust of traveling was upon me once again.

The following morning therefore found me at Rideout Bay which was the place we were to embark. There I found the guides engaged in loading two birch bark canoes. These were the first birch bark canoes that I had ever seen. Our guides' names were Robert Kah-ke-kay-inine (this meant Man Forever), the head guide and his son Thomas. They were in the first canoe. The other one was manned by John Mong-innine (which meant Loon Man after the northern diver bird called the loon) and John Atikoosebens (which meant Deer River).

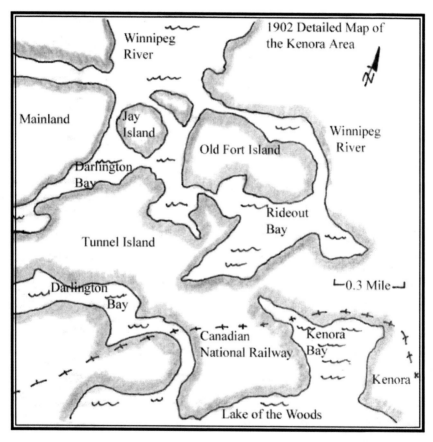

In due course the canoes were loaded with space left to accommodate the passengers, which were to ride in each canoe. As it happened I did not have long to wait before the manager's daughter, her aunt and a young nephew around the age of nine showed up ready to head back to the post. Their baggage plus a quantity of supplies for the post had already been loaded into the canoes before they arrived.

The Post Manager's younger daughter Eliza and I were to embark in one canoe and Mrs. Wix and her son Jonnie in the other one. As I was an unexpected passenger some difficulty was experienced in making room for me, however by shifting some of the cargo around, they managed to make a small space about two feet square in which I would have to fold myself up like a jack-knife, and most likely have my chin on my knees.

I stepped into one and was on the verge of seating myself on a thwart which was a strut placed crosswise, left to right in the canoe to brace it crosswise when one of the Indian guides nearby called out to me not to do so. He told me to get out of the canoe and he explained to me that these narrow strips of wood were not intended for seats but as a means of holding the two sides together. He also told me that the birch bark, not being too strong, could be damaged by sitting on them or if the canoe was resting on a rock of uneven surface.

Once everyone was in their designated spots and the guides seemed satisfied the canoes were pushed out into the water of the Winnipeg River. It was a beautiful one, with many deep bays and points of land and the shoreline, consisting mostly of pine trees, was smooth rock sloping gradually down to the waterline.

Alas, however, the day turned dull and the weather became unsettling. We hadn't gone far before it was pouring rain which made it not conducive to the enjoyment of the surrounding scenery and I was by no means comfortable either in the quarters assigned to me. I was thankful when the guides decided to pull into shore and make lunch.

Wanderlust

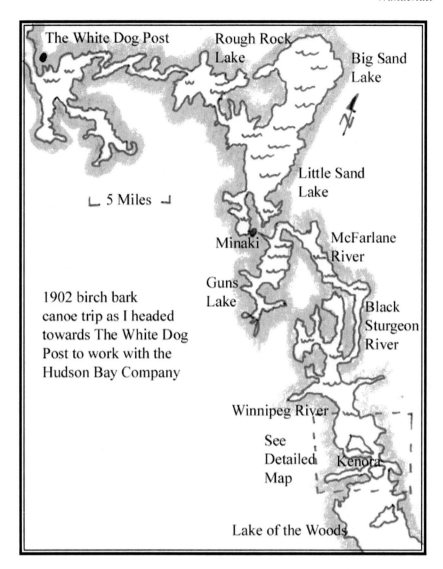

Seeing all the trees were wet and dripping, I could not help but wonder how they proposed to make a fire to boil the tea kettle. It seemed that it would be impossible with everything soaking wet but I was quite impressed to see one of the Natives gather some birch bark off a nearby tree which he pulled apart and lit with no trouble and then from the depths of a spruce tree picked up a handful of some very dry small twigs. Meanwhile, one of the other guides split up some dry gathered wood and in no time they had a roaring fire going by which we were able to dry ourselves whilst waiting for the kettle to boil and the bacon to cook.

We probably lost the better part of an hour all told before we were on our way again, but I did not really appreciate it until the weather cleared up and the sun came out. There it was, a shoreline of gently sloping rocks decked with stands of spruce and pine but for the most part it was pine with birch and poplar in their lighter shade of green.

Moose and red deer were plentiful I was told but it wasn't until we rounded a bend in the river that we saw a moose swimming across it. The guides proceeded to paddle as hard as they could, closing in enough that we were able to get a view of the moose as it paused taking a cursory glance at us. Then, it lost no time in disappearing into a thicket of alders, small twig-like trees growing close together. From then on I always wondered what would be around the next bend in the river.

After traveling some nine or ten miles we came to some rapids known as "The Dalles" but which were pronounced as the darls. Here the river narrowed down to some fifty feet in width and the current ran very swiftly between the high rocky shores. So swift was the water between the high cliffs that a small passenger boat operating on the river had some difficulty going upstream and it almost came to a stop in its battle with the current.

Whilst these rapids were very deep and comparatively free of rocks, there were strong whirlpools so we made our first portage here. The portage was a short one but I was astounded to see our guides carrying loads of three hundred pounds each by means of portage straps. These straps must have been around fifteen feet long and about three quarters of an inch wide, with a wider piece in the center of around two inches thick by eighteen inches wide which turned out to be the head strap that passed over the wearer's head.

It turned out that if a big load was being carried, a larger strap would be selected. The strap was tied around the cases in two places and the portager would be assisted by another person also carrying cases to swing the load onto his back and slipping the head strap over his forehead. Then one of the other guides would proceed to pile on more cases or maybe a sack of flour arranging the load so that the most comfortable piece came last behind the wearer's head. This served as a brace to keep the load from pulling his head back. Mrs. Wix told me that there were instances on record of men carrying up to eight hundred pounds for short distances.

The canoes were now carried, one man taking each end on his shoulder and carrying them right way up instead of upside down, which was the white man's method and was much easier. I learned that this was due to superstition on the part of the Indians, who presumably had visions of their canoe upsetting if they carried them upside down when on portages.

Unfortunately one of the guides dropped his end of the canoe rather suddenly and striking a broken limb on a log, cracked the birch bark canoe which necessitated a small repair job. They had however a small supply of pitch with them for just such an emergency and after heating it over a small fire the damage was repaired and we were once again on our way.

The weather had now cleared up and the sun was out and our journey would have been pleasant had it not been for the flies and mosquitoes. They told me that this was comparatively few compared to other parts of the country but none the less I found them abundant enough to annoy me.

On arriving at the north end of the lake and entering the river once more I noticed, as we rounded a large rock in the bend of the river, a rocky ledge on which plugs of tobacco had been placed by Indians coming upstream to placate the Manitou (their Great Spirit) in the hope that he would ensure them a fair wind or a safe journey across the body of water.

To me the scenery was magnificent and not being experienced in the use of a paddle I had nothing to do but sit still and admire it. I was however surprised to see such little animal life, as I had imagined the wilderness of northern Ontario to be teeming with wildlife. Actually I saw little but the occasional squirrel, a few blue jays and the occasional spruce hen or as it was correctly called, grouse.

It was evening time when we arrived at the falls where it was decided to make camp for the night. We were still some five miles from the post with four other portages to make and as the weather was deteriorating we decided to pitch camp before we came to another portage.

At this part of the river there was a large island about three miles long and a half mile wide, so we set up camp. Large clouds in the west were approaching, presaging a thunderstorm soon. Quickly the guides erected a tent for the lady passengers; the guides gave me a tarpaulin and cut a quantity of spruce and balsam brush for me to spread my bedding on. Having no experience, I simply used it as a top blanket. It wasn't long until we had a violent thunderstorm and the pouring rain soon made puddles in the folds of my tarp which in due course commenced leaking through, much to my discomfort.

Fortunately the ladies must have realized my predicament, for one of them called out and suggested that I better crawl into their tent. I was only too glad to accept their invitation as it stormed all night. In the morning it was decidedly chilly, the wind having veered off to the north and I was glad to find that the guides had quite a roaring fire going which enabled me to dry off my clothes to some extent while they were cooking breakfast.

What a breakfast it was, not that it was anything sumptuous consisting as it did of bacon, canned pork and beans which I washed down with innumerable cups of tea. It was the fact that this simple breakfast taken outdoors in the fresh air with the smell of pine in our noses and the distant roar of the rapids in our ears made it the most enjoyable meal I had ever eaten.

Breakfast finished, the eating and cooking utensils were taken down to the river and washed, the canoes were reloaded and once more we were on our way. From the camping ground to the next portage could not have been more than a mile away. There was no doubt as to why we hadn't camped there as there was no dry wood readily available and no place to pitch our tents. I was surprised to see that we had paddled nearly to the edge of the falls before landing to make a portage.

Falls and rapids had a great fascination for me and I would have liked to linger there but I had to forego that pleasure until another future time. The portage was made only around such parts of the falls as could not be safely run, and the lower end opened onto an eddy in the swift waters below the falls and these were easily navigable.

We had three other such portages to make in all before we arrived at the end of the island and the confluence of the two branches of the river. From there it was only a matter of two or three miles before we arrived at the White dog Post.

During my first canoe trip I was truly fascinated by the rapids, even though it's only natural for water to run downhill, as some Irishman remarked when he first saw Niagara Falls. However to me these rapids in their natural wild surrounding seemed different and more outstanding.

Chapter 8

The White Dog Post

PADDLING FOR ANOTHER few miles soon took us in sight of the White Dog Post which looked most picturesque sitting at the foot of a fair sized bay with an Anglican Church located nearby on an adjacent point. It was surrounded by green pastures with the bush in the background and in the foreground was a high bare rocky point with some three or four houses on top occupied by some French half-breeds (or Métis, as they now prefer to be called.)

On the side of the hill there were some thirty or so sleigh dogs, the property of some government survey parties. They paid these people to look after their dogs during the summer. Just which survey they had engaged in I'm not sure but I expect it must have been for the railroad through Minaki that was being worked on at that time.

On arriving at the post my first disappointment was in not seeing any furs around the house as I'd anticipated bearskin rugs and other types of fur. There were none in the store, the winter's harvest having all been directed to London, England a month or two before my arrival.

All the building except the canoe shed was constructed of logs which lay longitudinally with dovetailed corners and squared with a broad axe. The logs were chinked with clay and had been white-washed with paint and the roofs were of cedar shingles. The manager's dwelling consisted of two such buildings set at right angles to each other with a small connecting passageway which was large enough to include a small room that would become my bedroom.

The manager was a jovial, good- natured and very obese man whom the Natives nick-named "The Great Spirit Pig". Following my introduction to him, he explained my duties as "Clerk and Assistant" in detail to me.

First of all it was established that there were no set working hours as was established by the contract I'd signed. This indeed appeared reasonable. My duties during the summer months were to be up at seven a.m. light the kitchen stove and put on the porridge pot and the kettle to boil.

Whilst I was waiting for them to boil I would make a few trips to the end of the dock with two four gallon pails. With these I would fill up the large wooden barrels that sat along the back porch. This usually entailed four or five trips so I could suspend that operation long enough to make the porridge and have my breakfast. After finishing both these operations there was one cow to milk. Next I was to sweep out the store and have it opened by eight a.m. or as soon as possible. I would then remain there until the manager showed up around nine a.m.

If there were no customers around after his arrival, I'd have to cook for our team of four sleigh dogs. This involved cooking up four pounds of cornmeal with one pound of tallow in a four gallon cooking pot. Tallow was a rendered form of beef or mutton fat processed from suet which was mainly the hard fat found around the loins and kidneys. This tallow was mostly beef or mutton fat as it stayed solid at room temperature without the need for refrigeration to prevent decomposition.

The mixture was suspended on a rack over a fire built under it outdoors. Whilst waiting for the kettle to boil I'd keep occupied sawing up logs into stove lengths with a one man cross-cut saw.

Once the dogs were fed, if any of the Natives arrived at the store, I'd be called in to serve them. In order for me to be able to do so without an interpreter, as none of the Natives spoke any English, I started making up a list of the most needed words.

I started this the day I arrived and started learning words and phrases such as Kaygoonah-Do "You want anything?", and Aneeminik which meant "How much?" and of course the names of such commodities as flour, pork, tea, sugar, lard, baking powder and matches. All the basic necessities, as well as names of print items such as gingham, flannelette, and so on I kept adding to my list each day until it was not long before I could get along with a minimum of assistance. Store commodities of groceries were mainly in bulk and dispensed from barrels under the counter. Some of them containing dried apples and tea biscuits were emptied and were used to contain such other items as beans, split peas and sugar which came in bags.

The Anglican Church sat on a hill top with a few acres of pasture land, and there was at this time a resident minister and his wife. Unfortunately, for some reason unknown to me relations between my boss and them were strained. I was given to understand, following my first visit there, that I must refrain from further visits. I quickly decided to comply with these demands, crazy as they were.

The minister himself was an object of ridicule. Here is one of the stories that I heard.

When this man of cloth first arrived and the river froze over, he got the bright idea of heating up his poker in a fire. He then took this metal rod over a hundred yards to the river where he was going to thaw out a water hole. Of course, by the time he reached the river, the poker had gone cold. With the low temperature outside it would have been better for him to use an ice chisel.

Another story was that he brought to the store what he described as tailor's mink skins that he'd bought off some Indian. They were actually musquash which was probably just muskrat which, having no fur on its tail, was cut off by someone.

I mentioned previously of some houses at the entrance of the bay where the dogs were being cared for by Métis. One of them had four grown up sons with whom, along with some of the younger Natives, I used to enjoy playing football on the ice after the bay had frozen over. Whenever I could I would join in the fun which however only lasted a short time until the snow got too deep.

Across the river from the post was a rocky prominence along the shoreline with a sheer rock face and in the cracks flint arrowheads had been found. Interested as I was in such finds I was never fortunate to find any. I recollect that the river current ran pretty swiftly around that spot which for an amateur canoeist as I was at that time became much of a problem. The rock face was only attainable from the river. Possibly if I had landed some distance away and searched the top of the rock I'd have had a better chance.

On one occasion when thrusting my hand down into a barrel to get the large metal scoop, my hand encountered some foreign object. When I retrieved it, I found it to be a mink trap neatly set to nip my fingers. It was just a little joke by one of the Natives with the cognizance of the boss and luckily the trap had a weak spring but could have given quite a nip at that, so I was fortunate I didn't spring it.

My duties were indeed diverse; for instance, there was the time when the Indian Chief requested the boss for the use of my services in attempting to catch a large thoroughbred bull which had recently been bought for the Natives by the Department of Indian Affairs.

My boss put it up to me saying he had no objection if I cared to tackle it. I eagerly accepted and was called upon to place a noose over its horns which apparently the Natives had qualms about doing.

Actually there was no problem as I stood on one side of a rail fence and when the bull came over to investigate I simply dropped the noose over its horns. A number of the Natives grabbed the long rope and led it away to be slaughtered, so this turned out of course to be a crime seeing that the bull had been supplied to them for breeding purposes.

The Natives here also had a few Indian ponies, but this was the only place I had ever encountered them. To me they seemed to be pretty useless animals unable to haul more than a good dog team could. One of the Natives however owned a large white mare, not a pony. It was reputed that he thought more of his horse than his own wife. He would spend money on colored ribbons with which to decorate the mare but never for his wife.

Many of the Indians owned cattle; when they wanted to butcher some in the fall, they had quite a time trying to catch them as they wandered off into the bush. They even tried to snare them on the cattle trails, much as they would snare a rabbit. When not busy I'd ask for time off and join in an hour each day. I was returned the favor when one of the Native's grown up daughter took care of my laundry.

Occasionally some of the younger Natives would hold unique dances which never having seen before, I decided to attend and got so enthused that I tried to join in thereby causing some confusion. I earned a nickname for myself because of the way I danced; they called me "Kah-sah-sah-gon-de-bay-sed", meaning the head that bobs up and down. I was the tallest of the group which, coupled with my first attempts, apparently created this effect.

At other times the older people would put on a give away dance quite often, but these were incorrectly called a pow-wow. I went to one or two of these. The drummer, seated in the circle, would pound away, pom-pompom-pompom, meanwhile singing some song that went hi-hi-hi-ho or something like that.

The dancers, after first selecting their partner, would get up and hand them a gift. The Natives would bet with each other to see who would give the most expensive gift. They even gave such items as a rifle, a shotgun or dress material, in fact anything at all.

They would join the others forming one large circle capering around. Some of the men would deck themselves with fancy beadwork or silk work moccasins and strings of sleigh bells wound around their legs to jingle as they danced. These dances of course would take place in the open field or clearing if no field was available.

At some time during the dances or at some subsequent dance the gift-givers would be expected to return the favor by giving the donors something in exchange. When I joined in on one occasion, they gave away an old horse in exchange for a team of sleigh dogs. This deal had been pre-arranged and tokens were given to represent the actual gifts.

When winter came I was initiated into the art of fur buying and how to distinguish a muskrat pelt from a mink and various other types. The skunks of course I needed no experience in recognizing and of these there were many, some practically odorless (depending on how they'd been killed) to others that would nearly knock you down. Nevertheless, these were all strung up and hung upstairs in the store amongst all the other furs.

I was not of course allowed to buy any but could evaluate them and compare my evaluation with that of the manager. Most of the Indians left early in the fall for the distant points which were their hunting grounds, some going as far as eighty miles away and we would not see them again until Christmas or New Year. Others nearer by might come in once or twice before Christmas. With so many customers away during winter, much of my time was spent sawing wood, hauling it on a sleigh to the yard and piling it all along the side of the picket fence, and I used to take pride in the neatness of my piles of wood split up for the kitchen stove but which alas became an ammunition depot from which to chase stray dogs away, so then came spring and there was kitchen wood scattered all over the garden.

I'd go back to the store and the manager would often stay there until quite late at night, his office occupying one corner of the store but not enclosed in any way and he'd keep the store open quite late. He would tell me when I could knock off and go home. Whilst there were no Saturdays off or any half holidays, one could usually get a half day off by using a little good judgment and not asking for it if it looked like a busy day or if the boss was in a bad mood.

Spring came and I purchased a single barreled muzzle loading shotgun and a powder horn and I'd go out rambling through the woods shooting the odd partridges. On one occasion on coming out on a road I proceeded to follow one only to find after walking some distance that I was following it in the wrong direction, thereby adding considerably to my walk.

Another time I took a young Indian boy along with me and on coming out into a clearing we saw a log house with a bird sitting atop the stove pipe which protruded through the roof. It was suggested that I shoot at the bird; not realizing the house was inhabited, I went along with his suggestion. The following day a very indignant Native arrived at the store to complain to my boss. It appeared that the stove pipe became disconnected and deposited an accumulation of soot which had fallen into one of the rooms.

One day, running short of hay for the cow I was sent to haul a small load on a sleigh. This involved traversing some ice on the frozen bodies of water as far as it was safe and then following the shore around a point and up a small creek which was still solid. Well, I got my hay and was on the way home, when being overconfident I took to the ice on the bay sooner than I should have. I was going along fine and feeling relieved that I'd reached good sound ice when all of a sudden I dropped through in about ten or fifteen feet of water.

There on the not too distant shore stood the nine year old Native with his mouth agape or else he was hollering, if so I couldn't hear him. Fortunately, I was able to get out of the cold water, the ice being rough enough to obtain a handhold. I left the load of hay and it wasn't until the next day that an Indian went to retrieve it, taking two long pieces of wood and crawling on his hands and knees over the weak portion of the ice.

There was no doubt that the manager didn't realize that I'd no experience diagnosing the conditions of late spring ice. He, being a very corpulent sized man, had never walked any farther than from the house to the store as far as I recollect. The manager's family at the post consisted of his wife, a rather attractive daughter in her early twenties, a nine year old son, and another younger daughter. He had two other sons one of whom was home for his holidays from working on a survey party.

He'd stand around sometimes watching me sawing wood and give voice to some song that he parodied. I think it went something like "never, no never this white dog will be a hell of a place forever". I couldn't have agreed with him less, as I really liked the place.

I became quite enamored with the elder daughter, but alas she informed me that she had a fiancé in Winnipeg, Manitoba and of whom I became most violently jealous when he paid her a visit. She was however good company for me, and I became quite her confidant. We'd play card games or checkers in the evenings after her parents had retired and go skating when the conditions were favorable.

In the winter this daughter wanted to go to civilization where she had an uncle who was a bishop. He was probably of secondary importance in connection with her visit there. It was decided that I should go along and break the trail for the carryall in which she'd be riding. This vehicle consisted of a cariole (also spelled carriloe) which was a French word derived from the Latin carrus meaning vehicle. In this case it was a dog-drawn toboggan with a slanting back some two feet from the back end of the toboggan equipped with a back rest. Attached along the toboggan were parchment sides made of untanned moose hide and it was decorated with a painted design which extended to the hood of the toboggan. On this occasion the dogs were all suitably decorated with ribbons and pompoms.

Blankets were spread inside for the young lady so that she could ride in comparative comfort, this was of course providing the toboggan did not upset when going over the numerous hummocks which were mounds now covered with snow. Hummocks could be caused by plants, lumpy terrain, land that had an irregular shape or a fertile to a wooded area with a slight rise. I just thought of them as just another obstacle to go around. Sometimes the toboggan could upset on a sharp turn which was the job of the dog driver to prevent.

I'd never had a pair of snowshoes on in my life and so the day before, I was given a pair, explained about the harness which consisted of an inch wide lamp wick which we used for lighting up the cabin at night. I was somewhat leery as to whether I could accustom myself to the use of snowshoes on such short notice.

As things turned out, there was no occasion to use our snowshoes on this trip, as we found that there was a well beaten trail, the Indians in the area having made numerous trips to Kenora for supplies.

An Indian by the name of Atikosebens (Deer River) was hired to drive the sleigh running behind it holding on to a six or eight foot length of rope. By this method the toboggan could be guided to avoid colliding with trees or overturning while traveling around bends in the trail.

Kenora was around forty-six miles away and we were to make it in a day. I was told that on the lakes and the river I could ride on the short back portion of the carryall standing.

I therefore started out with what was known as a dog trot, and which I was able to maintain for some thirty miles or so, sometimes getting the occasional rest when the cariole upset or the dogs became tangled in their harness as frequently happened. There was also an hour's halt during dinner, by which time we had covered twenty-five miles and arrived at the village of Minaki which at that time was nothing but bush.

I noticed when we got on the lakes and river that old man Deer River kept hopping on the rear of the toboggan but I said nothing. After covering thirty miles however, my dog trot slowed down to a slow pace, and the dogs were pressing on my heels.

Shortly thereafter I was told by the driver that I'd have to travel faster than I was moving if we were to get to Kenora that night. Being exceedingly tired, this incensed me to the extent that I suggested that if I were not going fast enough then he should run ahead of the dogs and that it was I and not he who was to ride on the river and lakes. He thereupon stated that he had twisted his knee on one of the portages and that was the reason he was riding. This may have been the case, but then again he may have been malingering by exaggerating or fabricating a story to prevent the work.

Fortunately, when we were still some ten miles from Kenora, and it was getting quite dark, another Indian caught up to us with an empty toboggan and he suggested that I ride in it the rest of the way. Needless to say I was only too glad to accept his offer. I was very tired and the weather was cold.

The next morning I was really crippled up with muscle pains, and my legs and ankles were so stiff, I could do little more than limp around. It was fortunate that we were staying over for a day in Kenora. On my return to the post we were traveling back light and both Atikosebens and myself were able to ride, I in the carryall and he guiding it. When he did run behind hanging onto the rope, he occasionally, whether intentionally or not, let the carryall overturn and dump me in the snow.

When spring was well on its way I wrote to our District Manager complaining that my work was largely of a menial kind. I told him that I wasn't actually learning very much. Soon he paid an inspection and visited the post and he said he'd give me a post of my own on Sturgeon Lake, north of Ignace and here I would be the sole staff during the summer months.

Chapter 9

The Sturgeon Lake Post

There was a stern wheeled steamboat operating on Sturgeon Lake, Ontario in connection with the mining and prospecting activities going on in the Ignace area. Actually, there was only one producing gold mine there, the Sir Anthony Mine, situated about five miles north-west of the post on another arm of the lake.

Sturgeon Lake was a nice area and was located a little over a mile south of Tomiko in the Nipissing District of north-eastern Ontario. The lake flowed west through a channel around three hundred feet into Little Tomiko Lake. Here the Ontario Northland Railway from North Bay, Ontario to Cochrane, Ontario crossed that channel.

Ignace was a township in the Kenora District so it wasn't a long move for me. The Canadian Pacific Railway ran by it from the Port Arthur/Fort William area to Kenora. Ignace was located close to Sturgeon Lake which was on the shore of Agimak Lake. Here I soon found out that the town was named after Ignace Mentour by Sir Sandford Fleming in 1879. Ignace Mentour had been the key aboriginal guide through this region during Fleming's 1872 railway survey. During the time I was there around Ignace's early days there was a settlement of railway boxcars used by the English residents and they liked to call it "Little England".

Wanderlust

Just across from the post a couple of miles or so was a licensed hotel. The store itself was a newly built log building with a metal roof and quite up to date as regards to roofs in particular. The manager's quarters was a little log three room building with a pole roof made of logs split and the centre gouged out and laid alternately with split side up and vice-versa, forming a very effective roof.

As the Natives were all away during the summer months that I was there and being out of the route of traffic to and from the mines, white customers were very seldom. My existence there was rather a lonely one with a minimum of work to engage my attention and I was in fact a caretaker rather than a Post Manager in that respect.

Supplies on hand were few, but there was lots of fish and later on berries in abundance, so I didn't suffer from lack of food, even though it lacked somewhat in variety. By this time I'd acquired a minimum of experience in a canoe, and the only one there was nine feet long. The bow was so light that I had to weigh it down with large rocks, and by careful paddling from the stern of the canoe I could cross the lake and land at the hotel to pick up my mail. Not being a very experienced canoeist I was for some time just a strictly fair weather sailor.

During my brief stay there, one drowning accident occurred when two men started across to the post just a short time after I'd left the hotel for home. As to whether their bodies were ever found I don't remember. What I do remember were some fantastic suggestions as to how they could be located, something to do with floating a loaf of bread in the vicinity and which I think was some French superstition, there being many Frenchmen around.

Whilst at Sturgeon Lake I made the acquaintance of an Englishman who used to be on the Witwatersrand in South Africa. This area was a sedimentary range of hills which ran in an east-west direction at around six thousand feet above sea level. He said it was really geologically complex but the "Rand" as he called it was famous for containing forty percent of the gold ever mined from the earth.

The Englishman told me that he staked out a small island on which he had discovered two good veins of blue quartz, some of which ran thirty dollars to the ton, but more of this later, except to say I'd visit him at his log cottage which he kept as neat and attractive as any woman.

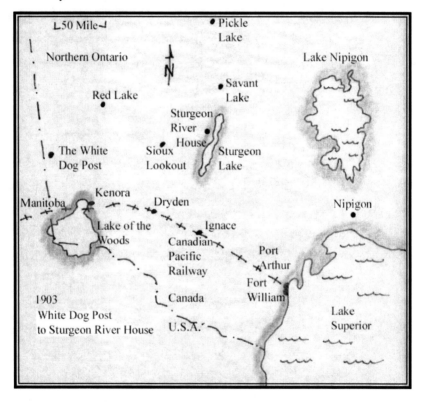

There was another incipient mine which was as far north as I knew, I think, up in Belmore Bay at the entrance to where the Long Bay outpost was.

One day I saw an Indian passing in a bark canoe, seated in the stern with a load of supplies. Evidently he had come from the hotel and was pretty light-headed as he was throwing his hat up in the air and shooting at it. That was the last anyone ever saw of him until his remains were found on a beach partly eaten by dogs it was said, but it could possibly have been wolves.

Speaking of dogs, I had been warned by my predecessor from whom I took over the post that they were a great nuisance and that his remedy was to load a gun using salt instead of shot and shoot them with that and they would never bother you again. It was not supposed to inflict any real injury on the dog. Well, I tried it once but presumably at too close quarters, for the dog let out a howl and I could hear it howling in the bush for a long time. It was getting dim out when I shot it and it was by then too dark to investigate. The next morning I found the poor beast and it seems the wad from the cartridge must have penetrated its hide and released its insides. It really did upset me for days and that was my last attempt to keep stray dogs away in that manner.

The new store was furnished with shelves on one side and along the back but the other wall across from the counter was just bare logs. It was just covered with white building paper and some man that came to take over from me for the winter got the bright idea for an hour's entertainment that we'd place large carpet tacks in the paper and see who could drive them in with a 22 bullet from the counter at the other end. It was good fun until it was discovered next spring that a canoe had been suspended outside on a bracket affixed to the wall and some of the bullets had missed the log backing, gone out in the space between the logs and through the canoe. Fortunately, however, there were only one or two holes resulting there from the shooting game.

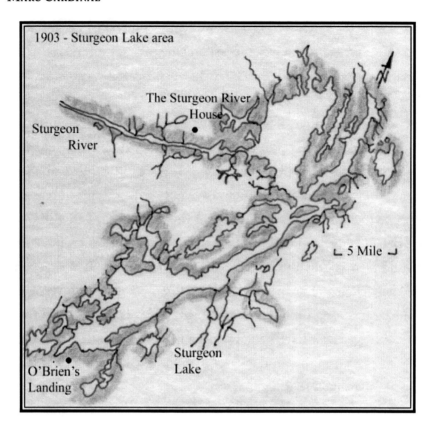

Chapter 10

The Lac Seul Post

I was next moved to Lac Seul Post, which was located on a large, crescent shaped lake in north-western Ontario. It was over one hundred and fifty miles long with a maximum depth of around one hundred and thirty feet. I was told that it was the second largest body of water entirely within the Province of Ontario. The lake consisted of bays, narrow channels and islands. This lake was mainly shallow and contained so many rock shoals that it was rich in walleye, northern pike, bass, perch and muskie. It must have been one of the best fishing areas in Ontario I thought.

This was near a town called Hudson which was originally called a "Rolling Portage" but was now a community located in the municipality of Sioux Lookout, Ontario. The Lac Seul Post was north of Hudson, and soon I was instructed to proceed to Dinorwic which was a small unincorporated settlement near Dryden, Ontario. Dinorwic was a few stations west of Ignace on the Canadian Pacific Railway where there was a Hudson Bay Post and it was here that I would get further instructions.

As there were some canoes leaving next morning I was to travel in one of them, but first we had an eight mile road to traverse by a horse team to a freight shed at our embarkation point. Then by canoe we crossed one end of Sandy Lake to the other and thence by river to Lake Minnitaki from where we had to portage for the third time, camping and spending the night.

During the evening we spent at Lost Lake, I was the guest of a young missionary student regarding whom the story was that, when he first held service at a small Indian Church, the hymns, not being sung loud enough to suit him, made him declare, "Give them hell boys!" In those days that was a shocking admonition for an incipient minister to make and in church at that.

Late in the evening a canoe arrived at Lac Seul Post with the bookkeeper and his family en route out for their holidays or so he'd been given to understand. He was therefore much perturbed to learn that I was apparently taking over his job. Unfortunately, that was something of which I hadn't been told, so I could possibly just be filling in. It turned out however that he was indeed being either let go or being transferred to another post. It seemed that the information he had received hadn't included this transfer. He seemed a very likeable chap during my short meeting with them.

The next morning there being lots of wild ducks around , the "missionary man" suggested he could borrow a gun from an Indian camped nearby and the both of us could go duck hunting for a couple of hours or so before proceeding on our journey. Alas, just as we were nearing shore some ducks passed directly overhead and in firing at them from rather an awkward position I lost my balance. We would have upset the canoe had it not been for the presence of mind of my friend in the stern who promptly flopped on his knees grabbing the gunwales. As it was, we filled up half of the canoe with water and in consequence had to paddle cautiously to the shore.

I had also, however, grabbed a gunwale with the shotgun in my hand which promptly slipped through my fingers and I watched as it sank in the deep water. Later on I went back to the spot in a fruitless effort to recover it and did not find it. I went to see the owner and promised him I'd arrange for a new gun for him on reaching the post. When I told the manager about it however, he said it was a gun given out on credit some years ago and he had never been paid for it. However, a promise must be kept so he said he'd order a cheap gun to replace the high priced one that I'd lost.

A letter in the mail that I obtained contained word of the illness of one of his young sons who was in Port Arthur, and as a result the manager's wife decided to leave the next day and spend the winter there. The manager decided that the both of us would occupy the new bookkeeper's house now recently vacated and take care of ourselves.

Well, at any rate, being a bachelor wasn't new to me, so I became cook for the light meals amongst my other duties while the manager hired an Indian girl to clean up and cook our dinners.

I had done a minimum of bookkeeping prior to this but here my duties were confined almost exclusively to assisting him in the office. There was also a small room off the office, containing carpenters' tools of which I made good use repairing mechanisms of guns or rifles that could be fixed with the use of a file, a vice and some rudimentary tools.

My proudest moment at such work was when with the aid of a small spike and a lot of hard filing I was able to make a new bolt for a Winchester 44 rifle for which I had only paid five dollars. Just how long it would have held up was questionable but it lasted for the short time that I was at this post.

The manager at the Lac Seul Post had a hobby of collecting the necks of loons, which he would skin and have tanned in some manner. Afterwards he would make them up into handles for ladies' handbags or other ornamental accessories.

When the lake was dead calm he and I would go out in a canoe and there would be two or three Indian canoes to go out in. The man in the bow had his gun to his shoulder ready to shoot instantly if the elusive loon bird diver surfaced, which could be from any direction. This afforded lots of sport for an hour or more, but should the wind get up the loon would take off on quick wings. Even a small ripple on the water could afford it sufficient means of hiding as the loon had only to put the top of its head out and would be down again into the water like a flash.

The Natives here were all Anglican and had a church on a point about a mile away from the post, the minister of which was a Cree Indian. At his mass he also spoke Ojibway, the language of his congregation there. On Sundays there was always a good turn-out of them, and they were good singers.

The minister and I would sometimes go hunting together and it was he who initiated me into the various methods of trapping muskrat and snaring bear, but whilst we set a bear snare we failed to catch one.

During the summer the Indians were paid their treaty money and their reserve being on the opposite shore, we brought over a quantity of goods transported there by canoe and then we would set up areas to trade in. This seemed rather unnecessary with the post so close by but it was explained to me that "free traders" as they were called would be peddling their goods there. So we also had to be there to compete with them, to get a part of the four dollars per head that they were paid in treaty money.

When New Year came around the Hudson Bay Company provided a New Year's dinner for the Natives which was held at one of the staff houses. Just what this consisted of I don't know but it certainly wasn't turkey, but probably moose meat and lots of bannock and tea by the gallon.

After the New Year, it was customary to send out a special shipment of furs purchased during the fall and this was the occasion of my next trip by dog team following my last excursion from The White Dog Post to Kenora. We were to go to Dinorwic, which was a small hamlet on the Canadian Pacific Railway and was roughly half way between Fort William and Kenora. On this trip we were to take out a shipment of furs and bring back the mail and supplies to Lac Seul Post. On this trip we took two toboggans, each one hauled by four dogs.

Our bedding consisted of one pair of seven pound grey wool blankets and a rabbit skin robe for each of us. The food consisted of flour, pork, tea, sugar, lard, baking powder and a few tins of pork and beans along with bully beef. For the dogs we had some twenty pounds of cornmeal, four pounds of tallow and a few fish.

A piece of canvas about four feet by eight feet was spread on the toboggans and the loads of furs along with the supplies needed were placed there and wrapped about with the canvas. Once the wrapping was done it was tightly secured by lacing a rope criss-crossed upward along the toboggan in the same manner as tying shoe laces. The grub box was placed at the end of the toboggan where it could be easily accessible without having to unlace the whole toboggan. The dog pail was placed at the front end, just behind the hood of the toboggan.

The distance being sixty miles, the trip could not be completed in one day this time and the trail necessitated the use of our snowshoes. The only exception to this was on some of the larger lakes, where the wind had packed down the snow hard enough to enable us to dispense with them. We found however that on most occasions when we discarded our snowshoes the crust on the snow was not of a consistent hardness. The result was that from time to time we broke through the crust. As we found this more tiring, constantly taking a step and breaking through the crust into the deep snow, we were glad to put them back on.

The weather was intensely cold and I had trouble in preventing my face from freezing when crossing the lakes in the face of a fairly strong wind. The temperature was around twenty-five below zero Fahrenheit, which would not have been bad were it not for the wind.

We covered some thirty-five miles that first day before camping for the night. This entailed shoveling out an area sufficiently large to accommodate us. To accomplish this, we took off our snowshoes and used these as shovels. Having done this, one of the Natives proceeded to cut a quantity of spruce and balsam brush which he spread to form a mat taking care not to cut any limbs that would be big enough to be felt through our blankets and add to our discomfort. I thought I could help but found that the greater part of my brush was rejected as being unsuitable. I also discovered that one did not just throw the brush around but laid it down in such a manner that the cut ends were inserted below each successive row.

Meantime two of the Natives were busy chopping down quite a huge supply of firewood, and I discovered that this, too, was no haphazard job, as certain types of wood were more suitable for firewood than others. I learned that dry poplar and pine were more suitable than others for firewood as they gave off a bright white flame that illuminated the entire camp. Spruce on the other hand was not popular owing to the fact that it tended to throw off sparks that would burn holes into one's clothing and bedding.

As there was lots of rotten poplar that could be pushed down without having to be cut, some of the branches were gathered to be thrown onto the fire before retiring and which smoldered all night. From this fire a modest heat was given off, but the benefit was in the morning when it could be fanned again after throwing on some dry wood. I was glad to see the Natives utilized some of the brush that I had cut and thrown at the base of a tree to which the dogs had been chained for the night.

One Native then went down to the lake and proceeded to chop a water hole to get the water for our kettle.

When this work was completed, the fire was started and the tea kettle and dog pails were placed thereon, and we proceeded to cook our evening meal which consisted of bacon, beans and bannock which was washed down with innumerable cups of tea.

Getting ready for bed, we grabbed our rabbit skin robes which were made by cutting the hides into long strips which were tied together forming a large rope that was woven into a thick rug to be used for our sleeping conditions. If one was wise the robes were covered with flannelette, but often the ones used were in their natural state and when the persons woke up in the morning they would find themselves with a mouthful of rabbit hair.

At the first glimpse of daybreak, the Indians, having been up already for an hour or more, would have the fire going. Upon rising we would perform our morning ablutions. This was done by digging some half melted snow, putting it on our hands with some soap, washing and then rinsing them off with water from the kettle; or, sometimes, someone would obligingly pour some of the water over our hands for us. Whether they were actually cleaner or dirtier when we were finished was questionable but at least we felt freshened up.

With breakfast finished, the toboggan loaded up and the dogs hitched, we were on our way at the break of dawn. It had been a cold night, around minus forty degrees Fahrenheit and the trees were all cracking with the frost as we pulled out. Gradually the stars paled out and the sun came up giving us some light but no heat. In fact the air actually felt colder and no doubt was, sunrise being actually the coldest part of the day.

At the end of the lake where the river was running too swiftly to freeze, clouds of vapor could be seen. Later in the morning the wind started to blow and I was mighty glad of the knitted Balaklava hood that I was wearing. It was like a long toque with an aperture on one side. This formed a hood which could be pulled down over the face and neck which left an aperture to see through and left the head and nose covered. The only drawback to covering the nose was the fact that one's breathing caused icicles to form.

The snowfall was much less as we progressed on our journey and we arrived at Savant Lake to find that the lake was all glare ice and the dog drivers were able to ride on top of their loads. In fact we all could have done so, had we had a good lead dog but none of our lead dogs would move unless someone was trotting ahead of them.

After an uneventful day we slept at some trapper's cabin at the south end of Sturgeon Lake and since the trapper only had his own small cot we all slept on the floor. With nothing but our rabbit skin robes which we put under us instead of using them as a cover we had a pretty hard bed. However, a bed of this kind necessitated continuous rolling and moving of the limbs and it gave the result that one did not awaken as stiff, just as if one had slept in comfort.

We were only fifteen miles from our destination, so we did not have to make a very early start in order to arrive there at Dinorwic, which was near Dryden. The return trip was made with ease as the trail had by now already been packed.

The following spring must have shattered all previous records for its lateness. This certainly confirmed the forecast of the manager who, when distant thunder was heard and thunderclouds seen in the south late in the month of March, predicted that that this was a sure sign of a late spring.

One morning, during the first walk in June following a heavy night's frost, "the missionary man" suggested to me that we go some eight miles down the lake to take up our muskrat traps. He assured me that owing to the heavy frost we could travel on the rotten ice going out but we would have to return through the bush once the sun was up.

This we accomplished without any adventure, but when the treaty party arrived in late June it was delayed for a few days by quantities of broken ice that had drifted to the outlet of the lake effectively blocking their passage.

Chapter 11

Vancouver, British Columbia

It was about this time that I got the wanderlust feeling again so I tendered my resignation and proceeded to Fort William from whence I took a special train to Vancouver, British Columbia traveling by day coach all the way. How uninteresting I found the prairies but was thrilled when the western foothills of the province of Alberta came into sight and that trip through the Rockies kept my eyes glued to the windows.

My arrival in Vancouver was equally thrilling for here I was back in England so it seemed. Gone was that resentment of Eastern Canada where I had heard or seen an advertisement for help on a farm stating "No Englishmen need apply". This of course was partly the fault of Englishmen trying to teach better methods as they thought, not realizing that it was not practical to adopt those methods over here, due to weather conditions, shorter growing seasons and much more. Even the stores here seemed to carry predominantly English merchandise which to me seemed strange seeing we were so much farther away.

I hadn't been there long before I secured a job as a receiving clerk at the counter of the Great North West Telegraph Office, where my duties consisted in receiving telegrams from customers. My job was counting the words and collecting payments from them. This resulted one day in my being summoned to appear in court as a witness in connection with some fraud case I think. In any case it involved the signature of a person and it seems I'd been given a telegram scribbled out on paper and had copied the same down including the signature for the party who handed it to me, he not being the sender of the telegram.

Fortunately owing to my youthful age I expect I was not seriously reprimanded, but the importance of never doing such a thing again was pointed out to me and never forgotten. Neither was the admonition I received on first entering the court house with wavering footsteps and my hat still on. To anyone who was as nervous as I was, having teasingly been warned by my fellow employees what I was in for, that "HATS OFF IN COURT" from the bench just about shattered me.

When I arrived in Vancouver I had noticed numerous signs stating the presence of many hundred Hindoos as they were called by some while others called them Hindu. It seemed to be a race of people of Persian origin as someone remarked while I was in the court room. They were probably Indian immigrants from India in Asia and their descendents had started coming over in the early 1800's and 1900's.

The problem was that many others were due to land on such a date and should we let them into the country? These Hindoos were in much evidence and a great many of them had been hired to work on the extra gangs on the railroads.

This was back in 1905 and I was around eighteen years old at the time. There was a great deal of unemployment then. At the time, I recollect, there was a parade or demonstration shortly before the boat was due to land and it got quite out of hand down in Chinatown. Windows were smashed and much damage resulted whilst the Chinese made themselves scarce. Eventually the fire department arrived and turned their hoses on the crowd and broke it up. Some of the bolder ones, however, then headed for a Japanese quarter where they received a very different reception being met by Japanese armed with broken bottles so the demonstrators eventually gave up. Unfortunately, some innocent whites en route home were attacked and hospitalized but none I think were killed.

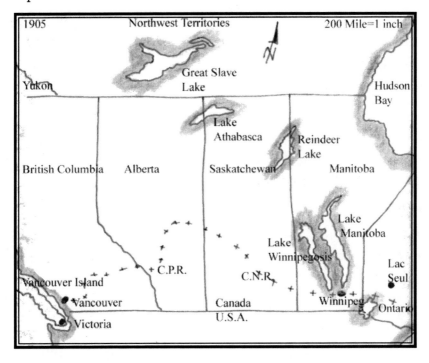

During my employment at the telegraph office, I got a half day off on Saturdays but only one Sunday in three. When the weather permitted I'd cross the Lion's Gate Bridge which was in the District of North Vancouver.

North Vancouver was separated from Vancouver by the Burrard Inlet and could only be accessed by the Lion's Gate Bridge, the Iron

Worker Memorial, the Second Narrows Crossing or the Sea Bus passenger ferry.

The area was bounded by the Capilano River to the west, Burrard Inlet to the south, and the Coast Mountains to the north. The scenery was nice with its rugged terrain and steep and winding roadways.

The Lion's Gate Bridge, officially known as the First Narrows Bridge was a suspension bridge and it crossed the Burrard Inlet connecting the two sections of Vancouver. The term "Lion's Gate" reflected the Lions, which were a pair of mountain peaks north of Vancouver. It was a long suspension bridge of around five thousand feet and I enjoyed crossing it when the chance came up.

I would cross the bridge and visit Capilano Canyon where the Capilano River flowed north to south and emptied into the Burrard Inlet. In the river it was interesting to watch the salmon run and the canyon water flow through the coastal rainforests. In its lower section it had a striking granite canyon with rock walls in excess of one hundred and twenty feet in some places. I would walk up the long plank walkway alongside the flumes specifically constructed to transport lumber, logs and shingle bolts.

During my stay there, a strike developed amongst the telegraph operators, but not being a member of any union, I continued to show up for work as that represented my sole slim means of livelihood. I had to bear being called a "scab" once or twice which was the worst that I had to put up with. I'm sure the work I was engaged in could have no bearing on it, or maybe it could if there were some scab operators receiving and sending which I believe there were.

Wanderlust

Anyway I soon was yearning to get back with the Hudson Bay Company and so I wrote an application to the nearest District Manager in Victoria, British Columbia. He subsequently had one of his inspectors drop in at the telegraph office to see me and he took me out to lunch with him so we could talk things over.

He informed me that the manager of a small post near Telegraph Creek in northern British Columbia had been drowned and the job would be open to me. He told me he would advise me later on when I should report to the District Manager in Victoria for further instructions; meantime I was to continue my present job.

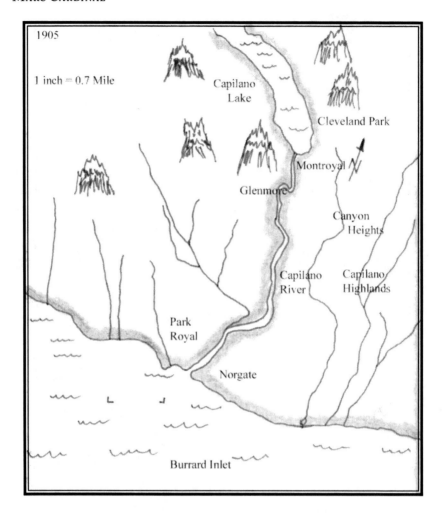

After waiting what I thought was a sufficient time without hearing from him, I foolishly quit my job and proceeded to Victoria to see the District Manager in person. I was then told by the manager that a prospector who had found the body or had witnessed the drowning had voluntarily undertaken to look after the Company's interest until such time as the Company could send in a new man. Apparently, the District Manager was so appreciative of what the man had done that he was offered the job which he accepted. Now, there were no vacancies and it was suggested that I go out and look for a job until such time as there would be one.

Not being able to find work around Victoria, I then took the train to a place called Sidney up north of Vancouver Island, and there I found a job as a bartender of all things in a small country hotel alongside a large sawmill. It seems the bartender had gone on a spree somewhere out of town and being long overdue, I was to take his place. Actually I was too young being only eighteen but I was easily able to pass myself off as being twenty-one. In those days I didn't drink and only smoked occasionally but I found that the smell of the liquor and cigars were too much for me. After a week, the hotel manager said he thought I'd better quit, not that he was displeased with my work but for my own good.

One amusing episode happened whilst I was being introduced to my duties. Sitting on the counter were three decanters with a chain around the necks and little silver labels indicating the contents, one of which at least I remember as being Peter Dawson. These I was instructed to replenish as needed from a large barrel in the rear, all being taken from the same barrel! It was amusing to hear customers insist on this brand or the other brand. They would even sample a different one to what they ordinarily drank, commenting on whether or not they liked it better!

From the hotel there was a view of the snowcapped peak of some mountain in Alaska. Whilst I was out walking one day I saw a flock of quail, the one and only time I can ever remember even having seen them.

I next proceeded back to Victoria on Vancouver Island where I secured a recommendation from the Hudson Bay Company office to the Hudson Bay Company wholesaler in Vancouver. I requested them to try and find employment for me of a temporary nature because the District Manager in Victoria had hopes of utilizing my services in the spring. Alas! They had nothing to offer, but sent me down to a nearby wholesale dry goods' store by the name of Grunshields. The manager there took me on as an employee, inexperienced as I was in that work, only to be informed a week or so later that an experienced man had applied for work and he had decided to avail himself of his services by putting him to work at my job.

Yes, there was a bad depression in those days and many highly qualified workers were willing to accept about any kind of work they could get.

I was not able to secure another job and was quickly running out of money so I decided to go to the Hudson Bay Company office once more and asked them to wire my former District Manager in Fort William. He immediately wired back to them instructing them to advance me my fare back, and one of the office staff was kind enough to loan me ten dollars as I didn't have any money, not even a cent.

Chapter 12

Jackfish to Longlac

On reporting to the District Manager in Fort William, Ontario I was assigned the job of looking after a horse they were shipping by freight to a small fishing village called Jackfish, Ontario. The town of Jackfish was located in northern Ontario and was situated on the north shore of Lake Superior just east of Terrace Bay.

When the last spike on the Canadian Pacific Railway track between Montréal and Winnipeg was driven in just west of Jackfish on May 16, 1885 it was said that one particular small section of railway cost seven hundred dollars. Jackfish had been established as a train order station on the Canadian Pacific Railway following a period of construction between 1883 and 1885.

Initially a siding or passing track was built at this location to allow east and west bound trains to operate on a single main line. At the train order station there was an electrical telegraph which enabled the station operator to control the movements of the trains with information received by the train dispatcher.

The town with its rocky shoreline became a port to receive coal and it also became one for commercial fishing. The fish caught here were packed in ice and loaded aboard trains bound for markets in Toronto and Montréal.

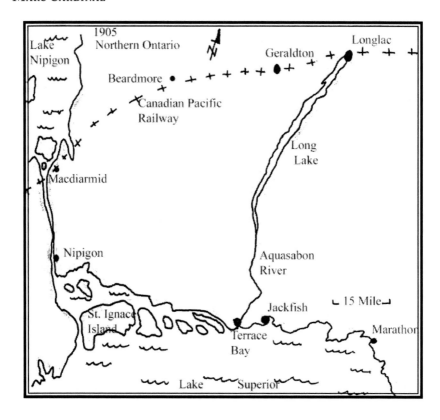

I was to ride in the caboose or as it was sometimes called the brake van or guard van which was coupled at the end of the freight train. Here I would sleep with the train crew and my job was to feed and water the horse en route to our destination. When I arrived there I was to deliver the horse to the small hotel where it would shortly be picked up and driven to Long Lake Post which would subsequently become known as Longlac Post.

There were a warehouse and a small shack some five miles or so west of the railroad to which I was to proceed and I stayed there in the company of a Frenchman by the name of Jean Bérubé. He was engaged to carry mail by dog team to the survey parties up north who were surveying for the Grand Truck Railway. I was to stay at this place until I received further instructions. I was notified at the railroad store that the freight for the Hudson Bay Company was at the Réveillon Frères Company warehouse and had arrived. I made arrangements with the agent to have the cars spotted for unloading at the warehouse. These had to be unloaded off the main line within an hour; otherwise, it would add to the cost.

Réveillon Frères or Brothers Réveillon as it was called in English was a French fur and luxury goods company with stores located in Paris, London, New York and Montréal. It was around 1903 that this company decided to set up a network of fur trading posts in northern Canada to compete with the Hudson Bay Company. They were fairly even at this time in competing, but I think that the Hudson Bay Company was still ahead.

The trouble was that one could not ascertain more than an hour or two in advance as to when we could have the train spotted. Since all the prospective helpers were fishermen, the problem was whether they would be available or not as they might be out fishing with their nets.

My luck was with me however and with the aid of many helpers we were able to get the sixty tons unloaded within the hour by just throwing it out more or less. So it was a good thing that the cases were strongly made and secured with scrap metal. It was a big relief to me when it was all safely stowed away in the warehouses which I had recently re-roofed by rolling the roofing down from the peak of the roof to the eaves instead of laterally.

Shortly after the arrival of the cases, the freighting contractors arrived with their six or seven teams. My duties consisted of making out the bills of lading.

The teamsters hauled their loads to a halfway place known as "Our Creek" where they made their camp. After taking the last load, I accompanied them through to the south end of Long Lake.

Going in with the first teams, just as we were coming out of the bush there on the ice, not a quarter of a mile from my future residence, was a pack of wolves. They had just run down a caribou and had eaten the greater portion when the sound of the sleigh bells scared them off. As there was a small bounty on their hides, I hoped they might return where I could shoot them right from the door of my shack. Unfortunately for me they never showed up again.

The accommodations here were by no means luxurious, as the sleeping quarters consisted of two pole bunks. Not that one slept on the bare poles of course but on a bale of hay which took the place of a mattress. Luckily I never did have any sort of experience with insomnia after a hard day's work. This was probably because of the hard work which consisted of sorting over and piling the loads of freight which were daily deposited outside the door.

I took great pride in piling all the cases and bales of assorted merchandise so that the numbers on each were clearly visible. This was in case any of these items were needed during the winter, and for which a team of horses and sleigh would be sent from the post some sixty miles north, and the case could easily be found and extracted from the piles.

My first dilemma occurred when, having piled a large quantity of flour bags at one end of the warehouse, on entering the next morning there they laid scattered all over the floor! Well, the teamsters were good heads, and on arrival later in the morning with their loads they all turned in and helped me restack the bags of flour, forty percent of which were probably in hundred pound weights.

Shortly after the freight was all in and sorted, the District Manager sent another young lad about my own age to assist me. He too was to remain there until open water as was his plan. I must say I wasn't too pleased when, as I was explaining to him the availability of any item, he remarked to hell with that. If anybody thought he would dig down to extract a case that might be at the bottom of the pile then that was a big joke.

It seemed to me that I would have to do all the work! However, it then occurred to me that the Native who accompanied the teamster could help me. One day, after my helper had arrived, a teamster came to take a load of some supplies to the post. He was accompanied by a Native with a dog sleigh who was always with him in case of trouble, and carried the great box on his sleigh.

Old Joe left bright and early next morning before we were up. We had just finished breakfast when the Indian helper came back asking if we had any rope as the team had broken through the ice in the narrows. We had no rope but decided we'd go along to see if we could help.

On arrival at the scene we noticed old Joe had one horse out and he suggested that we hang onto the short piece of rope some three feet long that he attached to the bridle. He suggested that we pull and not let him slip back in when the horse got its front feet on the ice. Actually, the water couldn't have been more than five feet deep but we didn't relish getting dragged in so we promptly let go when we thought it was wise. Then I reminded old Joe that he had chain in his sleigh. He said "By gosh, I forgot all about dat chain" and retrieved it from the sleigh and then we had no difficulty in having his first horse he'd rescued pull the other one out.

Fortunately it was a nice springlike day and after trotting the horses around for a while they were none the worse.

Old Joe then suggested that, the weather being so nice, we should accompany him and see the post where he was headed and which we'd never seen. I agreed, but my helper decided he'd go back to our domicile.

Later in the morning old Joe decided we could make a short detour to an Indian camp consisting of a few wigwams and boil our water in the kettle and have our lunch there. On arrival it was evident that there was liquor there, some white men having passed that way en route to the survey parties.

After lunch, our Indian guide suggested we could go ahead and he'd catch up with us as his dog team could travel much faster and so we did. After we had gone a distance of some miles I'd kept looking back to see if there was any sign of the Indian. Finally, when we were on a long wide stretch of the lake I told Old Joe that I could see someone but that he didn't appear to have any dog team. Old Joe, who was half- blind, assured me that he could see the dogs.

Well, he must have been "seeing things", for sure enough the Indian arrived minus his dogs; and, he was "pretty high". On asking him where they were he replied that he thought we had them. Well, there we were without any dogs!

Nearing camp at the halfway point there was a stable which could accommodate us as our sleeping quarters, but we had nothing in the way of food. We looked over our load and I found that we had a case of tea and another of "lunch tongues" but no flour or anything else. Also we had the cases and bales of hardware and dry goods. When we arrived at the halfway point, we hunted around and found an empty can which we boiled. After we decided that it was safe, we made our tea and drank it with our lunch tongues at supper and then once more for breakfast.

We had not gone very far the next morning before we noticed smoke over some far distant point on the opposite shore and indeed this point had already been named "Bukety" which means "hungry" point. Joe suggested we stop in the hopes of getting something to eat. We were fortunate in getting there before two mail carriers who were pulling out saw us headed their way and this aroused their curiosity. We headed off our course. They waited for us and made us some bannock and bacon to eat. We felt like new men and arrived at the post during early afternoon.

There I was berated for having left on our horse rescuing effort without putting on proper warm clothes. Luckily, the weather had stayed unseasonably warm. I was indeed fortunate that it hadn't turned extremely cold overnight.

At the post a new store was just on the verge of completion and was truly an exceptionally fine log building. The logs were all hewn and neatly dovetailed and the wall logs all had tapered and beveled slots near the centre where a tapered and beveled key was inserted to keep the logs from twisting or warping. The building was done by two Frenchmen and they could well be proud of it.

I noted too that the Company kept a few head of cattle at the time.

As for our Indian's dog team, I learned later that he apparently rolled off his sleigh when the dogs took off in pursuit of some animal. They had become entangled in the bush and were found dead. It was fortunate that our Indian must have retained enough of his senses to find us.

Chapter 13

The Nipigon Area

It wasn't long after this episode that I was transferred to Montezambert Post on the Canadian Pacific Railway west of White River and now known as Mobert. White River was a township located in northern Ontario and it was originally set up as a rail town in 1885.

Here I was sent to relieve the Post Manager who was away on a month's holidays. Little of interest occurred and my recreation consisted of walks in the bush hunting small game and one or two canoe trips on the river with an Indian who showed me the art of calling muskrat by making a squeaky noise with one's lips.

I remained there a few weeks after the manager's return and was then transferred to Nipigon on the Canadian Pacific Railway in the capacity of bookkeeper and assistant. Whilst I was accorded a substantial raise in wages, it transpired that I was actually a loser, having to pay for my own board.

Nipigon was another township in north-western Ontario and located on the most northern point of Lake Superior along the Nipigon River. It was south of small Lake Helen which ran between Lake Nipigon and Lake Superior. The bay was situated to the south and had several islands and was only about thirty to fifty miles away from the large body of water known as Lake Nipigon.

Interestingly, the Town of Nipigon was named after the crater on the Planet Mars which was named Nipigon Crater or as some called it Crater Nipigon.

Nipigon was a comparatively small place at that time, but in the process of rapid growth, and during my brief stay there the first concrete block buildings were being built. The blocks were being made by a small hand machine.

In addition to my bookkeeping activities, I was required to relieve clerks in the store during their lunch hours and, as this entailed selling liquor at times, I found that this was rather confusing.

At that time no Indian receiving treaty money was allowed to buy liquor and that was the law, but some of our customers had every appearance of being Indians but were non-treaty Indians. These non-treaty Indians could therefore be served whilst others apparently white were actually classified as treaty Indians. These were the offspring of a white mother and an Indian father, a Métis.

I therefore ran the risk of offending my customers or being hauled up in courts until such time as their standings had been made known to me as they carried no identification as to whether or not they were treaty residents or non-treaty residents.

For recreation here I used to go trout fishing with some of the clerks who would get the loan of a handcar and four of us would pump the handles to drive the five miles or so to a small creek where the brook trout fishing was good.

A handcar, also known as a pump trolley, a pump car, a jigger or a kalamazoo, was a rail car powered by its passengers, or by people pushing the car from behind. It was mostly used for maintenance of train tracks or as a mining car. Here we used it for passenger service to get closer to the lake without walking the long distance. It had the typical design which consisted of an arm that pivots, seesaw-like on a base which we pushed up and down to move the car. If we heard a train coming we just had to lift it up and take it off the tracks and then put it back on once the train had passed.

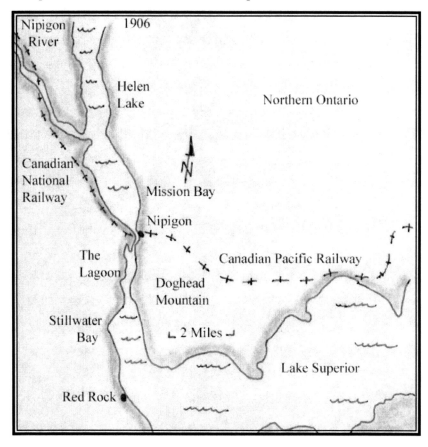

Occasionally, I'd go fishing off the banks of the Nipigon River, world famous for record breaking speckled trout, but it was only occasionally that I could catch one much over a pound in weight. It was important, I had been told, that an understanding of how moving water shaped the stream channel could improve your chances of finding trout. In most streams, the current created a riffle-run-pool pattern that repeated itself over and over. A deep pool could hold a brown trout, but rainbows and smaller browns were most likely found in runs. Riffles were where you found small trout, called troutlet, during the day and then the larger trout would crowd in during the morning and evening for feeding periods.

There was also a pool room in the village where I first tried my hand at pool, but I never became very proficient at it and I don't think I ever gave it much of a chance later on.

There was one storekeeper here with quite a large store for the size of this community. It was reported that he started up in business there during the railroad construction with a half dozen colored bandana kerchiefs. It was interesting as I had heard of handkerchiefs but never gave them much thought. Well his kerchiefs were apparently much in demand, and his turnover so rapid that he soon was able to acquire other items and in due course build and establish his own store.

We talked about it and he explained to me that kerchief was from the French word couvre-chef which meant to "cover the head" and it was a triangular or square piece of cloth that was tied around the head or the neck for protective or decorative purposes. Another kind of kerchief he explained was a bandanna (or bandana) which he told me was taken from the Hindi word which meant "to tie" and was a type of colorful kerchief, which was usually worn on the head. On the other hand a handkerchief or hanky primarily referred to napkins made of cloth, used to dab away perspiration and clear the nostrils. Sometimes in Victorian days it was a means of flirtation for a woman who would intentionally drop a dainty square of lacy embroidered fabric to give a favored man a chance to pick it up. This would give him an excuse to speak to her while returning it.

Well he told me there were other uses such as blocking odors while walking on the street or using it around the face to keep the dust from being breathed in while working on some dirty job.

I was also quite intrigued to learn that one of the Natives was an illegitimate son of a French Count who subsequently left him sixty thousand dollars. This Native's brother, also living there, was a deserter from the United States Navy.

Chapter 14

Sugared Fish and Watered Down Milk

I WAS ONLY at Nipigon some four or five months when I received word that I was being transferred to the Osnaburgh House on the north end of Lac St. Joseph. This entailed another railroad journey to Dinorwic and thence to Lac Seul, but in this case we followed a different route from my previous trip. We followed the English River from Minnitaki Lake, only skirting the east end of Lac Seul and thence following a small stream known as the Root River to a portage into Lac St. Joseph.

On this trip I went in with two birch bark canoes which picked up loads of freight at the Company's warehouse near Dinorwic. It was comparatively early in the fall, in October as I recollect and I hadn't made much preparation for the trip in the way of warm gloves and was in fact wearing light woolen ones in which the fingers had holes. These were made that way with the last finger joint uncovered and were in use in England from whence my sister had sent these to me as a gift. I think we used them in England when picking blackberries partly to protect our hands from the thorns.

Well, the weather turned cold and we had snow and sharp frosts and I never suffered so much. I had in fact to keep my hands in my pockets, instead of being able to help paddle. Lac St. Joseph was a large body of water located in north-western Ontario and was mainly accessed by the town of Ignace.

The closest town was Pickle Lake, which was a great place for animal watching as a person had many opportunities in that area to view moose, woodland caribou, timber wolf, black bear, game birds, bald eagles, song birds and many migratory birds such as ducks and geese. It was a popular destination place for fishing and hunting and was referred to as the gateway to Ontario's "Last Frontier" because of its remote location. The community was located on Pickle Lake, from which it had gotten its name.

The portage into Lac St. Joseph was quite long and when we set out on our trip up the lake there was a pretty stiff breeze as we came out into a large bay which we had to cross. The Natives decided they'd wait for the wind to let up. The other canoe, which was some distance ahead, made the crossing before the wind got too strong. It was dark when we reached the dock at the post.

The manager, named Jabez Williams, from Cornwall, England met us at the dock quite incensed. He was anxious to know how come the other canoe had arrived a few hours earlier and also where our load was. He glanced into the canoe and asked me if I considered the canoe to be fully loaded?

All I could reply was that, as he could see for himself, there was no room for anything else even though it was riding a bit high in the water.

I discovered later that his big grievance was that we'd failed to bring along his case of liquor, the contents of which I'd not been advised. The next morning he took me to the canoe shed to get my suggestion as to how large a canoe he should send to pick up the rest of the supplies we had left. Jabez didn't like my suggestion, and sent a smaller one. Meantime the manager at Lac Seul post, having learned that there was still freight at the warehouse for us and with the weather freezing, sent a large Lac Seul freighter with a capacity of a ton and a half to take the goods up to us.

I must admit it gave me a boost when it arrived almost loaded to capacity. I'm sure old Jabez' spirits welcomed the arrival of his missing items.

Shortly after that, whilst I was out in the store, an old man who helped there called out that he didn't know what had happened to Jabez, but he'd fallen down and couldn't get up. Well, if I didn't know any better I was sure by now that his missing items had something to do with Jabez falling down. We managed to get him over to the house where his wife could look after him in his drunkenly state.

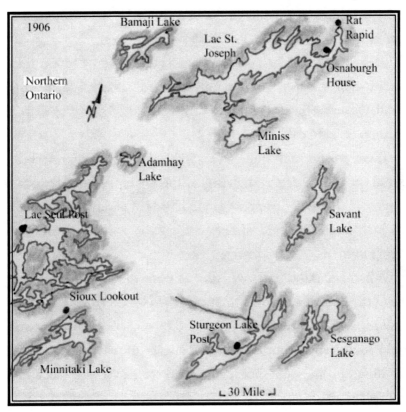

At this store there was a bell in a small tower that had to be rung at seven a.m. to arouse the outside employees and again at noon and at six p.m. Pertaining to our store, sundry meant the many diverse and various items procured in our business. The word could mean lots like toiletries and other usually small items of no large value that were too numerous to mention. It was stuff that would be found in department and hardware stores, drugstores and markets.

The outside workers were engaged in making sleighs or toboggans, snowshoes, looking after and repairing canoes and such like tasks, and whatever we could think of for them.

At this post, I found the food pretty hard to take. It consisted largely of salted fish which hadn't been properly done I'd imagine. Anyway, it smelt to high heaven and completely killed one's appetite! The milk was so watered down as to be hardly distinguishable from water.

It developed later that I was responsible to some extent for the condition of the fish. I mistakenly shipped a bag of sugar instead of salt to our outpost where the fish were salted down in kegs and returned to us to eat.

There was however quite an assortment of delicacies reserved for special occasions such as the visits of the District Managers and the Inspectors. These consisted of canned birds of various kinds, the like of which I'd never heard of before. Quail or pheasant I think were among them.

When late fall came, I was glad to learn that I could accompany one of the outside help on a trapping trip. He was to set traps for the manager who had frozen his toes and having had them amputated could no longer wear snowshoes and engage in that pastime. We had two different lines, one occupying the better part of a day and the other just half a day.

Both of us carried 22 caliber rifles and on one of the trips we saw a fisher following a rabbit trail across a lake. We could see both the rabbit and the fisher and so we took in the chase, hoping to get a shot at the fisher. The going was tough in the deep snow and by the time we got within range we were both so winded that we could not hold our rifles steadily enough. I missed, whereupon the fisher sped for the nearest shore while my companion yelled his head off. On enquiring why, he stated the fisher might in his state take to a tree to which we could track him, but the fisher didn't oblige us.

The shorter half day trip I attended myself and I heard that there was a timber wolf around with a missing paw that had followed my trail one night. The wolf would remove the brush from the top of the little pens, pull out the stakes at the back of them and eat the bait, leaving the trap undisturbed at the entrance to the pens. This he did to all the traps it visited.

One day, the wolf's tracks being fresh, the boss suggested we'd try and run it down. He thought that, with only three paws, it would not go too fast. However, the wolf took to a dense thicket in the bush and we had to give up.

On another occasion when crossing the lake I saw on the far shore what appeared to be a pack of wolves and I'd heard they might follow but never attack a man. I must say I was relieved to find it was a mirage, or optical illusion which caused a number of prairie chickens to appear greatly enlarged.

It was in December, 1906 that we started out by dog team from Osnaburgh House on Lac St. Joseph to head out to the Hudson Bay Company trading post on Sturgeon Lake to bring in the Christmas mail and supplies as were needed for the Christmas season. Our party consisted of four Indians and me along with three toboggans. Ordinarily our party would normally consist of three Indians and myself, one Indian to each toboggan; but, owing to the fact that there was no trail broken and it looked to be around two feet of loose snow, the task of breaking trail alone would have been exhausting. The Indian who was to assist me went by the name of Skunk.

The two of us walked ahead of the dog teams which as well as being less exhaustive also made for a better beaten trail for the dogs. Jabez estimated it would take us ten days for the round trip and we were provisioned accordingly.

Provisions for this trip consisted of flour, baking powder, tea, sugar, lard and pork along with some bacon and butter for me as I preferred it to lard. In addition I used to carry a good supply of baking powder buns liberally reinforced with raisins and lard (the latter was used to keep the buns from freezing).

After a very heavy going over long portages we arrived at Puhkokagan Lake about noon and stopped along the shore for our dinner. The dogs were in their harnesses on the ice while the Indians cut a liberal supply of spruce or balsam boughs as both were good and they spread them out like a mat on the windward side of the fire. This was so that we could eat in comfort without the wind blowing the smoke in our eyes.

I learned useful points when making a fire outdoors. You had to know the direction the wind was blowing from, a point of reference which in this case was the fire, where to build it, and the area which lined up with the wind direction and the fire. Windward was the direction from which the wind was blowing at the time and leeward was the direction downwind from the point of reference. It took some judgment to determine which way the wind would blow as an adjacent knoll may well appear to be on the leeward side of where the fire was located, which is the smoky side, but when the wind hit the ground the smoky side could easily be reversed.

Whilst some of the Indians were thus engaged, others would be cutting dry wood for the party while another would be chopping a hole through the ice for water with which to make tea. These jobs having all been accomplished the Indians would pick up a bough and brush the loose snow off their moccasins so that the heat from the fire would not melt the snow and dampen their footwear.

As they had made their bannock before leaving for the noon lunch all that remained was to fry the bacon and make the tea. Believe me when you are cold and hungry, bacon, bannock and tea taste mighty good. Whilst we were waiting for the tea pail to boil I amused myself taking shots at a Whiskeyjack bird sitting on a limb.

I shot it and one of my team drivers, a Scotch Métis, told me I'd surely break my rifle as it was unlucky to shoot at it. Later on during the trip I got into deep slush and, using the rifle to tap my snowshoes and knock the slush off, I broke the stock whereupon I remarked to Sandy that he was right about the Wiskeyjack. Sandy, being a very religious chap said, "No, it was because it was on a Sunday that you did it."

After filling our pipes and having a brief smoke we were ready to start out again. During our lunch one of the dogs had not been idle and had amused itself by chewing through the traces of its harness. I'd noticed that dogs were habitually addicted to such tricks. Of course this made necessary a minor repair job which was accomplished by boring holes through the cut pieces of leather with a pocketknife and connecting them with a piece of twine.

During the afternoon, whilst crossing a small lake, we, the trail breakers, got into some deep slush which made for a hasty retreat and a detour around it. Meanwhile our snowshoes became heavily laden with a mixture of slush and snow. Taking them off and tapping them together disposed of some of the excess weight and as soon as we came back to the bush we broke some sticks. Continually we knocked the snow-slush mixture off our snowshoes with the stick as we walked and it helped to lighten their weight. Thank goodness we hadn't gotten our feet wet, other than on the outside of the moccasins or it would have been necessary to make a fire and either dry or change our footgear. If not we would have frozen our feet and probably not known about it until it was too late.

A moccasin was a shoe that was made of deerskin or another type of soft leather and it consisted of a sole and sides made of one piece of leather which was stitched together at the top and sometimes came with a vamp which was an additional piece of leather. The sole was soft and flexible while the upper part was often adorned with embroidery, beading or something unique. We had heard of numerous instances of people freezing their feet in this manner and knowing nothing of it until they went to take their socks off, with the result that they had to have their toes amputated.

Shortly after this we came upon some fresh snowshoe tracks and the dogs perked up their ears and started to run with the result that we could not walk fast enough to keep the lead dog from stepping on the tail end of our snowshoes and tripping us. The drivers tried to hold them back by pulling back on the tail rope of the toboggans but with little success.

We soon came in sight of an Indian encampment consisting of three wigwams; the occupants, on hearing our dogs barking, were soon outside to see who their visitors were. These people were friends of our Indian dog drivers so we were invited in for a cup of tea which in this case was a bowl of tea. I've always known the Natives to have a pot of tea handy and they drank it out of tin shanty bowls or small milk pans. They suggested that we stay there for the night but, since it was only mid-afternoon, I insisted that we continue on our journey in spite of their pleas.

Actually they had a good reason for camping there so early and had they told me I would have consented to making camp. Apparently there was no good camping spot for quite a few miles as we soon saw that the countryside had been burnt out with nothing left but small jack pines. It wasn't until moonlight before we eventually found a suitable spot. We decided where the most sheltered location was and we made sure that there was lots of dry wood and brush for a fire and bedding. Only then did we proceed to set up camp.

As usual we used our snowshoes as shovels to clear away the snow over an area large enough to accommodate our party. Poles were then cut and placed some three feet apart and at an angle of forty-five degrees. The hessian covers were taken off the toboggans (these were the covers used to wrap the load up in) and placed across the poles to make a windbreak. A large quantity of brush was then cut and spread out over the shoveled out area and quite a large pile of wood was cut. As usual we were careful with our judgment about the type of wood for fuel.

The dogs now unhitched were bedded down first, so we cut down some brush where they were chained so that they could sleep in comparative comfort curled up on the brush separating them from the cold snow beneath. The dog kettles which were about a ten quart in size were then hung over the fire and their feed cooked. When this mixture was ready, it was poured out onto the snow in front of each dog that would start gingerly eating around the edges, sometimes shaking its head when it got a mouthful that was too hot.

Having taken care of the dogs, the Indians now proceeded to make their bannock which entailed mixing in some flour and baking powder and lard in a tin milk pan. They would assemble it into some form of a cake with as little kneading as possible and would place it in the frying pan which was then stood up on its edge more or less in front of the fire.

Sometimes, the Indians would vary this by frying the dough in lots of lard which looked like some sort of doughnut that to me was highly indigestible.

After supper, the snowshoes were stood up at a safe enough distance from the fire to enable them to dry without burning the babiche, this being a type of cord, lacing, rawhide or sinew that was traditionally used by the American Indians. The wet moccasins and socks were hung on a willow to dry and we stood around the fire turning around once in a while to heat our backs as we filled our pipes and enjoyed the quiet of the night with a little conversation.

We spread our blankets and rabbit skin robes, as we had no eiderdowns and used our overcoats as pillows and we turned in to sleep. Sleep did I say? Well the Indians slept but as for me I laid awake most of the night shivering and counting the hours until the Indians would be getting up to start the fire.

Arriving at Savant Lake roughly halfway on our journey we were pleasantly surprised to find a minimum of snow on the ground; and as a result, we completed our round trip in a week. Arriving home after dark, the boss, still being in his office, concluded there was something wrong. His first ejaculation to me was "What's the matter? Why did you turn back?" as he hadn't expected us until two or three days later.

There was another trading post run by some private firm some five miles or so away. The manager whose name was Frank had at one time been a good friend of Jabez, but he was now a bitter enemy, so much so in fact that old Jabez refused to let his small steamboat land at the dock.

Frank had recently acquired a new clerk and assistant by the name of Rupert Clough who turned out to be my missionary friend from Lost Lake. He and I decided we'd try to rekindle the friendship between our respective managers. The hostilities were the result of a New Year's Day prank. As it was reported to me it came about in the following manner.

Old Jabez had gone over to his rival Frank's place on a friendly New Year visit during which they both had a few too many drinks. Old Jabez went out to the outside toilet and was comfortably seated there, if that was possible in subzero weather, when there was a tremendous crash, accompanied by the report of a gun.

Jabez was convinced that Frank was trying to kill him. Actually it was all a prank, Rupert hurling a rock or some heavy object at the flimsy outhouse whilst Frank fired off a shot gun.

In spite of Jabez' antagonism, however, he didn't try to stop me from visiting there. I learned from both parties that they would never speak to each other again until the other party apologized. So what Rupert and I did was lie to our respective bosses by saying that we'd been asked to convey the other's apologies. It worked and we were glad to be able to bring them back together again.

Jabez had four or five children by his second wife who was a Native. He had decided to give them all names the Indians couldn't pronounce properly. He therefore named one Christopher which became Curnistopen to the Indians and then there was Charlotte who became Sharnot, the Indians having no L sound, and so on down the line. His reason for doing this must have been just another of his idiosyncrasies no doubt.

Later on in the winter I had to make a second trip to Sturgeon Lake for supplies and this time a rather amusing episode happened.

It was a Sunday. We arrived at Sturgeon Lake where I was put up overnight by the manager in the new dwelling. During the course of the evening a contractor for some construction work dropped in. He proceeded to pull out a bottle of rye from his jacket and explained how he'd been able to obtain it on a Sunday, the bar being closed. That is to say, a heavy board shutter was lowered and locked, but the bar room itself was open.

The contractor, having noticed the shutter did not cover the space between the ceiling joists, went out and cut a long pole to the end of which he attached a snare. By looking through the cracks between the boards and inserting the pole between the joists, he was able to snare the bottles. I forget how many he claimed to have snared, but anyway he went back and paid for them the next morning for as he said it was only a joke, plus perhaps he had the thirst.

Going back to my trip, I'd started out with a pair of snowshoes in which the cross bars were too closely spaced for me with the result that my heel would touch the rear bar and cause much pain. However, I could not do without them.

I began to realize how agonizing a bastinado must be. A bastinado was a corporal form of punishment where the soles of the feet were whipped until terrible pain was felt, and at the moment I sort of felt what it must feel like.

Foot whipping was called many things such as bastinado, falanga and falaka and was a form of torture where the human feet were beaten with an object such as a cane, a piece of wood or a whip. It was a favored form of punishment, and, although extremely painful, would hardly leave any marks.

Fortunately, when we arrived at Savant Lake there was a small outpost where I was able to exchange them for a larger pair. We had a pretty tough trip back to the post as I'd overloaded the toboggans by allowing over a hundred pounds per dog which was what I'd been told constituted a load. Well, that might be all right on the lakes or hard beaten trails, but not for the going we encountered and as a result the Indians had to cut poles and push from behind to assist the dogs.

On arrival at the post I was warmly commended by Jabez as being the first clerk he'd had that could bring in a decent load. So I suggested he'd better thank my dog drivers as they practically had to push all the way. He went on to tell me about one of his former clerks, who forgot to carry enough dog food and had to feed his dogs cheese of which they consumed all of it and were spoiled animals afterwards.

He even went on to say I was the best clerk he'd ever had excepting of course for one grown-up son from his first wife, who also froze his feet and had to have his toes amputated.

This was a year prior to Jabez suffering likewise which was funny seeing that he'd berated his son for being so foolish as not to dry out his footwear after he'd got them soaked. Then he did the very same thing himself the following year, when on coming home from his trap line he mentioned to his wife that he'd got some slush on his moccasins. She told him he must have frozen his feet. He poo poo'd the idea, but discovered on taking off his footwear that such indeed was the case.

Chapter 15

Resignation, Prospecting & Duluth, Minnesota – 1908

It was whilst at Osnaburgh Post, which was also known as New Osnaburgh, Osnaburgh House or Oz for short, which was in the Mishkeegogamang First Nation that I attained my twenty-first birthday. I had recently inherited a small sum of money from my grandfather's estate and I decided to take a trip home to England and forthwith tendered my resignation.

I went out by way of Sturgeon Lake, however, and spent a few days with my prospector friend there whom I had talked about before from South Africa. He suggested that I put my money into his claims from which I would undoubtedly reap a large profit in the near future.

I did invest in his claims, spending a month or two with him and doing some prospecting whereby getting some knowledge regarding gold bearing rocks. Suffice to say that I never did take that trip to England.

There was a big gold rush on at the time and some quite spectacular specimens of gold in the white quartz were often taken to a jeweler to be converted into such decorative items as tie pins, brooches and much more. We often visited various prospectors on their claims that had some blue and white quartz.

The veins of quartz on our property were all blue quartz. It was there that I had my first experience in blasting operations holding the metal spike whilst my partner swung the sledgehammer. I was just praying he wouldn't miss, which of course he didn't.

There was lots of visible gold on some of the claims we staked. They consisted mostly of pockets and in those that did carry any appreciable lengths of veins we found that the gold average was too low to be marketable.

On the other hand, on others claims, no gold was visible to the naked eye but apparently was present like dust when the rock was crushed using a pestle and mortar and panning it showed a very good clearly visible deposit. In fact it averaged thirty dollars to the ton which was a very rich find. At that time, it was known as free milling ore. Unfortunately, it was our bad luck that too much of the gold would be lost in the tailings to make it a paying proposition.

After spending a few months with this prospector, I decided to go to Duluth which was a port city in the State of Minnesota, down in the United States of America and was the Seat of St. Louis County. It was originally inhabited by people of the Paleo Indian Tribe, and was originally named "Keegewaquampe" which roughly meant people among the great hill.

Duluth's geography was dominated by a rather steep hill which was a transition from the elevation of Lake Superior's beach. It was sometimes called the San Francisco of the mid-west; this was referring to the Californian city's similar position on the hill, leading down to a busy harbor.

Here I obtained work at Gasser's Grocery Store on the main street where it was customary to display barrels of apples out on the pavement. It became part of my job, rolling them out in the morning and bringing them back in in the evenings. Here I also learnt the importance of extreme accuracy in weighing, when the manager walked over to me as I was weighing out some lumps of sugar and removed one or two cubes. He explained to me how soon such inaccurate weighing could eliminate what minimum of profit they could make on such items.

As I recollect, I was not very popular with my fellow employees because I was opposed to taking out citizenship papers, as they thought I should, seeing I was making my livelihood there.

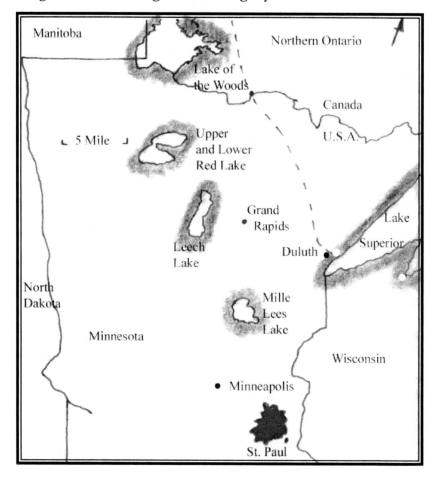

Subsequently, I was given the job of collector of what I was told were very bad accounts, and I remember having to try and collect from a manager of a hardware store who even threatened to shoot me. I recollect no pointing of a gun at me, but I wasn't taking chances and made a somewhat hasty exit. On reporting the incident to the manager, he agreed there was no point in my calling on him again.

There was an inclined railway where one could take a ride to the top of the steep slope on the Dover Stretches on which the city was built. Sometimes I'd take a ride to the top and then take long walks into the countryside.

There were also two parks I used to visit. The first one, Lester Park, was near the city's center and had a small stream running through it, the banks of which were all built up with stones, giving it a very artificial look.

The second park, which was called Lincoln Park, was much more to my liking. It was in one of the larger neighborhoods in the city of Duluth, Minnesota. It was situated between Garfield Avenue to the ore docks at Carleton Street and 34th Avenue West.

This neighborhood named the "West End" by the Duluthians, stretched up the hillside to the Skyline Park Road. It was a beautiful area with a waterway called Miller Creek flowing through it.

Lake Superior of course was not far away and whilst I used to pay it the occasional visit, I had no recollections of the place whatsoever other than having to cross some bridge to get there.

Chapter 16

The Call of the Wild Once More

With the advent of winter came the call of the wild once more, so I returned to Port Arthur and thence to Fort William to see what prospects, if any, I had in getting back in the service of The Hudson Bay Company. Port Arthur was next to Fort William in the Thunder Bay District.

The Government of Canada was determined in the late 1850's to begin the exploration and development of western Canada. Confederation happened in 1867 and Simon James Dawson was employed by the Canadian Department of Public Works to construct a road and route from this area on Lake Superior to the Red River Colony, on the west side of Lake Winnipeg in Manitoba.

The Department of Public Works had a depot on Lake Superior where they stored their supplies. This area acquired its name in May, 1870 when Colonel Garnet Wolseley named the tiny fire-ravaged settlement Prince Arthur's Landing in honor of Prince Arthur, who was the Duke of Connaught and Strathearn and was the son of Queen Victoria.

Prince Arthur was serving with his regiment in Montréal at that time. In 1871, the Ontario government surveyed Prince Arthur's Landing Town Plot which officially confirmed the name and opened the land for legal possession. It soon prospered from the Canadian Railway construction boom during 1882 to 1885 and the Town of Port Arthur was then incorporated in March, 1884 which was one year after acquiring its new name.

I was glad to find that the welcome mat awaited me and I was now back on a three year contract and was to be sent to Nipigon House on the east shore of Lake Nipigon, some fifty miles or so north from the town of Nipigon, where I'd previously been employed.

From there I was to start out and travel in the company of a number of men who were being taken by team to work on railroad construction work some ten or fifteen miles north of the post. When I say taken by team, this does not mean that they rode; they just trailed along behind sleighs.

As I recollect, the weather was quite severe and some of us had a hard time to keep our nose and ears from freezing.

The men had a minimum of food apparently on the trip, although they were being charged a dollar each, much to their indignation. I had my own lunch which I'd procured at our overnight stop at the foot of the lake, where I'd joined the party.

I was to find out that Lake Nipigon was the largest lake that was entirely within the boundaries of the province of Ontario, the five other great lakes like Lake Ontario being split between the United States of America and Canada. So I started calling Lake Nipigon the sixth great lake. It eventually drained itself into the Nipigon River and headed towards Nipigon Bay and then into Lake Superior where were situated Fort William and Port Arthur.

The lake was noted for its towering cliffs and unusually green-black sand beaches that were composed of a dark green mineral which I found out was called pyroxene. The only thing that impressed me about the lake was the large pressure ridges the like of which I'd never seen before.

We arrived at the post late in the afternoon, the contractors and their men continuing on the remaining ten miles to their camp. Here then was to be my quarters for the next three years or so under the old Bikney Islander by the name of Donald Murchison who was manager of the post. He too was married to an Indian woman and had three youngsters consisting of a boy and two girls.

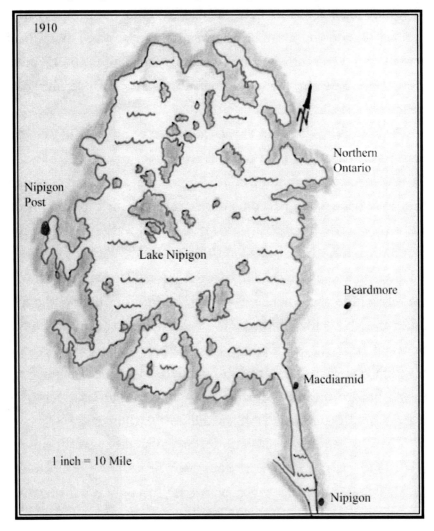

The buildings here were widely scattered, some hundred feet distant, the trading store being down near the lakeshore with the warehouse, from which were sold such commodities as flour, pork, lard and tallow. The dwelling house was located on top of a hill and entailed the climbing of close to fifty steps or even more.

During the winter it was not allowed that the stove should be lit except for a day or two before Christmas when it was very busy. The excuse given to me was that should the place burn down it would result in great hardship for all the Indians within a fifty mile radius.

We therefore stayed in the house where we had our office and kept a lookout for any customers heading for the store. I'd don my mackinaw and mitts and go to wait on them in the store, and suffering as I always had from bad circulation it was agonizing to have to take off my mitts and measure out cotton print in subzero temperature.

I found it still cold even in my mackinaw which was a heavy dense water repellent woolen cloth and I had heard that these jackets were invented by the Métis women in 1811, when John Askin, who was an early trader on the Upper Great Lakes , asked them to design and sew woolen jackets for the army. Most likely the name Mackinaw came from the Strait of Mackinaw which was in Michigan, U.S.A. This area was an important trade artery during the 1700's and 1800's. It just might have been that this heavy woolen cloth traded through this area became known as Mackinaw cloth.

If one had to weigh out salt pork, one had to walk to the warehouse and grab a hook to fish the slabs of fat back out of the kegs of brine. I discovered, after many frustrating efforts, that the easiest way to get the tallow from the huge, heavy tins when it was frozen solid was to chisel it out.

Salt curing was one of the oldest techniques known for curing meat. The pork was packed in salt and was continually turned around for six months. As it cured, the water was drawn out of the meat and the salt penetrated inwards. This prevented molding and rotting, acting as a preservative to keep the bacteria from living inside of the meat. If it was well handled the salt pork could last a year or more and was packed in barrels and made it a huge staple food in many areas of the world.

Sometimes I'd be on my way back to the warmth of the house when one or two other customers would show up and I think I can truthfully say I never suffered so much as I did serving customers in that unheated store.

At this post our wood was all hauled in by a bull, not by an ox, as was the case at White Dog Post. Our bull here was quite small in comparison of the White Dog ox, but seemed quite docile in his harness consisting of an old fashioned wooden yoke. This was a wooden beam which was usually used between a pair of ox to allow them to pull a load. I heard later that a pair of oxen was called a yoke of oxen and if you were working with them you were said to yoke a pair of oxen.

Donald, coming as he did from the Bikneys, was an ardent fisherman, with the net that is. I doubt if he did any angling in his life. During late fall, I used to accompany him in the freight canoe when he went to set his nets and also when he went to see them, and I'd help him extract the fish. When we got home, I'd have to stab the fish through the tail with what was known as a spearing knife, push sticks through them, then hang them up in batches of ten on an outside rack made for that purpose.

Most of these fish would eventually be used for dog feed during the winter, but some that were hung, consisting mostly of whitefish, were also used for our meals after the really cold weather set in.

After the lake froze, Donald explained that we'd set nets under the ice using a tarpaulin for a windbreak, so I suggested we put up a small tent with a camp stove in it right over the hole, from which we pulled our net. I was sure glad he went along with the idea!

The Native method of setting nets under the ice was to cut as long a pole as could be found to the end of which a cord was attached. Inserting the pole through the main hole and knowing the length, another Native would take a forked pole, and, with his axe, chop a small hole big enough to insert his pole; and, catching the long pole in the fork of his stick, would keep pushing it along in the required direction until he reached the end. Meantime, his helper would go ahead and repeat the process until the length of the net had been reached, then the net was attached to the rope and driven through.

Sounds simple, but only if it was set under clear ice when the location of the pole was visible under it, but not so easy if there was any snow on the ice. Well, even in the comfort of the tent I found the job of untangling the fish net frustrating and one was sorely tempted to break the mesh sometimes.

At the time, back in 1910, I guess, I was around twenty-three years old, which I remember as being the date of Halley's Comet being visible. It was one of the most famous of the period comets and could be seen every seventy-five years or so. Some comets could be brighter and this short-period one could be clearly seen with the human eye.

It was around April 20, 1910 and the comet was notable for several reasons; it was the first close approach of which photographs existed and it was a spectacular sight. I also heard that the comet could in fact have been what was then called the Great Daylight Comet of 1910 which was supposed to surpass Halley in brilliance and actually was visible in broad daylight for a short period of around four months before Halley made its appearance. Whichever it was, it was really something to see.

The Lake Nipigon whitefish were very good to eat, but it didn't take long to get tired of fish served fried for breakfast, boiled for dinner and fried for supper day in and day out, and week in and week out, too, excepting for the odd time we'd have rabbit. However, the manager had little use for this type of game; as he said, there was little or no sustenance in them.

Witness, he told me, the Indians from Nipigon on the railroad who subsisted largely on fish and were all well built and robust compared to those who came from the north of us and subsisted largely on rabbits and moose meat and who were for the most part skinny individuals.

When Christmas rolled around it was customary here to give all our Natives a dinner in the house kitchen in relays; it was also the custom that the manager and the clerk stand at the door and welcome the braves with a handshake and the women folk (regardless of age) with a kiss, which was quite an ordeal in the case of the more repulsive–looking ones.

On New Year's day, the Natives used to go from house to house to visit their own kin and eat at every house they visited, just staying long enough to eat, regardless of the time of the day, before moving onto the next house. The Natives here were all Roman Catholics and had a white framed church on an island known as Jackfish Island a mile or so from their reserve on the mainland; the island itself or part of it was also a native Reserve on which there were a number of Native log houses.

On one occasion, during my stay at the post, the Natives, who were very superstitious, all moved across to the island as they claimed there was a Mon-soo-Kahn around who was throwing stones on their roofs and who would kill them if he caught them in the bush, and consequently they were afraid to go in there. The Mon-soo-Kahn was supposed to be some wild spirit. I explained to them that I took frequent walks in the bush and had neither seen nor heard any sign of it, but I was told that, being a white man, I was immune and would not be molested. I forget how long it was that the rumor lasted but I think it was about two weeks.

During my three year sojourn there, our freight was all brought in by steamboat which were steam powered boats and they mainly worked on the lakes and rivers. Well, there were also keelboats and steam scows, the difference being a keelboat was safer but only good in deep waters while the scow had a flatter bottom and could be used for going easily into shallow water near the shores to unload supplies.

There were two in the area, one a large steam scow owned by the Réveillon Brothers who had a trading post across the lake and had the scow for transporting supplies for the coming railroad, as well as a passenger boat, the S.S. Sabika.

The freight first had to be transported overland from Lake Helen. Teams would also pass near the post transporting supplies as well as bringing in the workmen and their baggage.

Late one exceedingly cold day, something like minus twenty degrees Fahrenheit along with a strong wind, a team or two arrived, asking for shelter overnight. The contractor and his teamsters were accommodated in our house and the laborers (nearly all foreigners), in a building known as the Indian shack, ordinarily used to sell, and containing nothing in the way of bunks. So, these men had to sleep on the floor and, having no food, were supplied by us with tea biscuits, sourbelly and beans, corned beef and of course tea and sugar, and were left to rustle for themselves.

Poor beggars! Many of them had no suitable footwear and we heard that one or two had to have their feet amputated. Exposed parts of the body were easily affected by the cold.

Bright and early the next morning they were all on their way for a further ten miles to their first camp at Wabanoosh Bay.

This same Indian shack served a number of unforeseen purposes. It once served as a temporary ward for an insane woman until such time as the police could come and get her!

This also provided the occasion for my services being called upon, as whilst there was an Indian constable living on the reserve at Jackfish Island, the Natives for some reason didn't want to request his help. I think it was due to some relationship with the demented woman and him; and so, there being a pair of handcuffs at the post, it was suggested to Donald that he give them to me and that I should go to the wigwam where this woman was staying, only a half a mile or so away. Then I was to try and engage her in a conversation and while talking to her slip the handcuffs on her. Then, I would get her out to the Indian shack. All went well and was accomplished without having to resort to force.

Having gotten her in the shack I felt sorry for her so I went to the store nearby and got some apples and oranges which I gave her. When the police arrived two days later to take her away the Natives had decided that she seemed all right again and they wouldn't let her go. The police were quite understandably indignant on being called on a wild goose chase and said that , if they had any more trouble with her, not to bother calling them. I think it wasn't too long after this event that I was transferred again so I don't know what happened to her afterwards.

Whilst there was not much hunting to any extent here, if at all, in the spring some of the Natives would anchor to fish off the shore of an island, immediately opposite the post. From the point of the island, they would shoot at the seagulls that came to swoop in after the fish. They never shot any adults; but the brown gulls, which were the young ones and which it was therefore assumed hadn't lived long enough to regale themselves on any floating corpses, were shot because they were considered fit to eat.

I expect shooting sea gulls was strictly against the law, from which however the Natives considered themselves exempt and there was no one around to enforce the law anyways.

We had a large potato patch and Donald told me he never had any trouble getting help to dig it up, as there was a rumor that some Hudson Bay Company Post Manager who died there had a cash box of his savings buried in that area. Nobody knew exactly where but it was supposed to exist.

Sometimes I wonder if that canny old Scotchman didn't invent the whole story to ensure diggers (to which the Natives seemed strongly averse) being available when needed.

Whilst at Nipigon House there was no canoe available for my use except a birch bark one which, owing to it being unseaworthy, wasn't used by anybody. Profiting of my experience on Sturgeon Lake, I thought I'd give it a tryout with a real heavy rock for ballast; and, I found it to be safe enough in reasonably calm weather. To those who have never used a birch bark canoe, I'd point out that you had to make some allowances for the wind when heading for a certain spot, as the wind would blow the canoe sideways just about as fast as you progressed forwards.

One interesting job I was assigned to in 1910 was taking a census of the Native population at a lake some fifty miles or more north of the post, which entailed quite a number of portages and for which I was supplied with a freight canoe and crew of two as we were also taking in some supplies to the Natives camped there.

The Natives there were illiterate, nor could they speak or understand English, and the vast number of questions I had to ask them was absurd, seeing that they kept no written records of their catches of various kinds of fish and fur, number of game killed and other such information.

Also, they appeared to be equally ignorant of their ages, some looking as if they were thirty or forty and giving their ages as fifty or sixty, which at the time seemed to me absurd, but from more recent experience with Natives who were in a position to know their own ages, it leads me to wonder if indeed those ages I doubted might not have been correct.

Whilst at this encampment I saw a primitive way of cooking fish for the first time. The Natives would simply stick a long pointed willow branch down the dead fish's throat and stand it up to roast around the open fire outside and when cooked would eat the flesh leaving the intestines intact, instead of cleaning the fish prior to cooking.

En route home, I undertook to carry the bow end of the canoe over one of the portages and foolishly put one of my fingers through the mooring ring in the inverted canoe as I carried my end on my shoulder. Slipping on a piece of clay that I'd mistaken for a rock, I fell and, not being able to extract my finger in time, the whole weight of my end of the canoe fell on the back of my hand causing severe pain and a lump as big as a ping pong ball, which prevented me from assisting in the paddling but caused no permanent injury.

Chapter 17

Manager of the White Dog Post

IN 1911, AFTER serving three years at the Nipigon House Post, I was transferred once again to White Dog Post, but this time in the capacity of manager. Instead of going in via Kenora, I took the recently constructed railroad to Minaki at the entrance to the south end of Sandy Lake. During my absence Minaki had become a tourist resort and boasted quite a large tourist hotel. My recollections however of the trip in from Minaki are nil, so it must indeed have been uneventful. Apart from the growth of the Village of Minaki, the scenery from there on to the post was undisturbed.

I had no assistant in the store other than a French Métis by the name of John Savier whose duties were much the same as I'd previously been engaged in when I had first worked there. John also worked as interpreter when the conversation extended beyond the limits of my vocabulary.

John also had much more experience in the proper method of baling furs which at this post was accomplished by the use of a long heavy log the end being inserted in a rope loop. It acted as a lever with which to pry down the lid of the press. One or two men would then put their entire weight on the other end of the log in an effort to squeeze the bale into as small a bundle as possible.

This post was the best for country produce. There was an abundance of wild rice which in turn ensured the visitation of large flocks of migrating ducks and geese. Both moose and deer were also plentiful, and also various forms of birds known as grouse but were more commonly referred to in the area as birch or spruce partridge although they were not partridge.

There were little or no blueberries in the near vicinity, but lots of raspberries and even wild plums along with hazelnuts, the only post at which I ever found these.

The Natives would pick the plums when still green, put them in a box and bury it underground where they would ripen, but these did not have anything like the flavor of sun-ripened fruit. The Natives would then take these to Kenora and sell them.

Fishing wasn't too good here, but there were sturgeon in the river, one of which we caught on a line set for us by my Outpost Manager, and which weighed seventy pounds and must have been close to five feet long. I carried it ashore over my back with its head slightly above my shoulders and its tail touching the ground!

We had not envisioned a catch of such magnitude and, nearly all the Natives having left for the summer to go blueberry picking or whatever, there was only one family left so we asked them to smoke it for us but unfortunately they only smoked it lightly and the bulk of it was wasted.

The method used in catching sturgeons was by the use of a long length of cod line to which were attached shorter lines of eighteen feet or so which had cod hooks, each of which had been touched up with a file to make it needle sharp. These lines were attached to the main line at four inch intervals and, at every few feet; there was a longer line with a weight attached should the length of it be carried by the current. In this way it was possible to dangle the fishing line about a foot or maybe even lower from the bottom of our fishing area. These hooks were not baited and the sturgeon, which is a bottom feeder, would get snagged by one or two hooks. If he thrashed around, he would be snagged by many more.

It was of course quite a trick setting such a line but our instructor used a wash tub, placing each hook along the rim and there were up to two hundred of them.

He also warned us to take a club along when lifting the line as we were using a small canoe. This was very sound advice for a seventy pound sturgeon thrashing around could easily have upset us, had we not clubbed it to death or insensibility first.

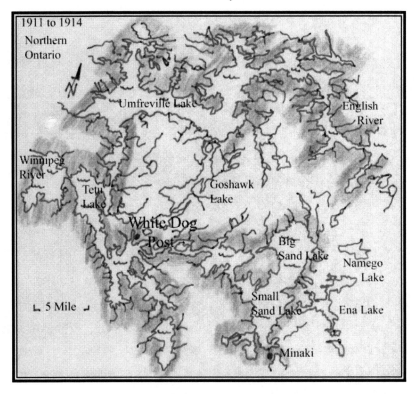

Thank goodness there was only that one sturgeon, but what a task it was preparing the line! We were told however that there was another method entailing much less work but it necessitated baiting each of the hooks. With this method there were less hooks but the bait had to be changed daily as the sturgeon would not otherwise take it. However, having no bait, we ruled out that much easier method.

In August, 1912, at the age of twenty-five years old I decided to get married to a woman I knew whose name was Eliza. I had met her on my first trip into the White Dog Post back in 1902. She had been the younger daughter of the manager at the time and, having been enamored by her older sister, hadn't paid much attention to her. There was an Anglican Church at the post known as the Islington Mission. It was there that we were married and our honeymoon consisted of a short vacation in Winnipeg.

During our stay at The White Dog Post, we had a varied assortment of pets, consisting of a bear cub, a red fox, and a large owl; however, we did not have them all at the same time.

The bear cub was just a few weeks old when it was given to us by a Native who had trapped its mother. The first day that we had the cub, we left it in the house whilst my wife Eliza and I went for a walk and, on our return, we discovered it had pulled down the curtains, possibly trying to climb them and generally upsetting everything it came into contact with; so, we made a pen for the cub outdoors.

The bear was still on a milk diet which of course consisted of canned milk, and should the milk not be mixed to its liking it would put its paw under the basin and dump it all out, meantime making a hissing sound. We only kept it for a month or two before giving it away to a tourist.

Our red fox had to be kept outside in a cage too; and, becoming very malodorous and not showing any evidence of making a good pet, we decided to let it go.

As for the owl, which was just a young one, it became quite tame and would come and go as it pleased through the open door of the kitchen. One day, the owl didn't come back and, as I recollect, was gone for a week or two, and we had decided that it had left us for good. But no, the owl was back again. Then one morning, following a severe thunderstorm during the night, we found it laying dead in the yard, having possibly been buffeted by a high gust of wind against one of the buildings. I wasn't sure of the type of this owl, but the Natives called it Coo Coo Cachool.

I had no pet dogs, other than the sleigh dogs, but my helper had a snow white long haired mongrel which went by the name of Shanz whose appearance was often sought after when taking pictures of White Dog Post.

Regarding the name of the post I had been told by various people, whether on good authority or not I cannot say, that the place acquired its name from an old Native custom of eating white dogs during their festive ceremonies.

During my second year at White Dog I bought a pony, not an Indian pony, but one that was capable of hauling a decent load and it would be used for trips to Kenora.

I also acquired an outboard motor which I think was one of the first to come on the market, and the name of which I have forgotten. Some of our Natives were very good at building boats, having in earlier days built pointers for freighting in supplies, so I got them to build a boat for my outboard. Alas, neither of us realized the limited horsepower of the motor and when the boat was completed we discovered it would only attain a maximum speed of four or five miles per hour.

Nevertheless, I was bound to make a trip to Kenora, and we navigated the Dalles rapids by tracking the boat from the shore. One man with a pole stayed in the boat to fend it off any rocks, the river being low at the time. It was fortunate he knew how to handle the job as he came very near to being dumped out when he got caught in a cross current that very nearly capsized the boat. No doubt my complete inexperience in tracking up a rapid may have contributed to the hazard.

During the spring and fall large flocks of waibus and geese could be seen migrating and would become the target of any Native who had a rifle handy, although the chance of hitting any was, as a rule, remote, as they were usually flying very high; however, on one occasion, my helper dashed into the store, grabbed an old Swiss Army rifle of around 50 caliber and started firing; and, sure enough, he hit one which was seen to plummet into the bush across the river some quarter of a mile away.

Jumping into a canoe we went in search of it and probably would never have found it, had it not been for the clamor of the flock. The goose had been shot through the neck of all places; the odds of it happening, at the height it was flying must have been fantastic!

Whilst on the subject of wild fowl, one of the Natives shot a swan on one occasion and gave us some of what used to be regarded as the food of kings, but not having all the ingredients which were no doubt added by his majesty's chef, we found it to be no better than a goose.

During the summer of that year, John's family went to a small hamlet by the name of Malachi where there was an abundance of blueberries. It seems there developed some trouble between the railroad section gang and John's sons, one being struck on the forehead by a stone and knocked unconscious for a short time. This event caused them to move back home to the White Dog Post.

It wasn't too long after the incident that the son died and John asked me if I would conduct the burial service since the missionary was absent. John assured me that it had nothing to do with the blow to the head that he had received, but from some other illness. In my ignorance of such matters I agreed to do so without any qualms, and it was not until some months later when I was in Kenora in the Hudson Bay Company store there, that I was accosted by what turned out to be the coroner who took me to task for not having reported the fracas at Malachi and having performed the burial without first obtaining a burial permit.

Insofar as burial permits go, I'm sure that in those days, at such remote and isolated places, these must have been dispensed with so all I could do was state that the man's father had given me to understand his death was the result of illness. I got off with a warning while in Kenora and I learned another lesson about the environment that I was living in.

Whilst on the subject of burials, I might add that most of the graves were not adorned with flowers but with colored ribbons or some personal item of the deceased; in the case of a child, possibly a doll or some other type of toy would be placed on the grave.

Not so were the graves at a nearby reserve at Swan Lake where the Natives were for the most part pagan and there on a hillside were their graves, each covered with a miniature replica of a house. It gave the graveyard the appearance of a small village of miniature houses and was the only one of its kind I ever encountered.

It was on a visit to Swan Lake one time when I heard that a medicine man who lived there was to treat some Native for what I think was rheumatic pains and I decided I'd like to witness the procedure if a white man was allowed to do so. They told me that there would be no problem with this. Incidentally the medicine man's name was "Wimitigoosh" which means white man. Well, his hair was snow white anyway.

On entering his wigwam, I found it in total darkness so all I could do was listen. Well, he diagnosed the sickness as being caused by some worm or bug and called for the help of "maymays" (the red pennated woodpeckers) to extract the worm, at the same time making a very pleasurable imitation of the woodpecker's call in reply to his pleas. Of course, not being sufficiently versed in the Native tongue this was all explained to me afterwards by my bilingual friend who accompanied me.

Actually, what I referred to as a wigwam was in this case a "wah gen ooh gahn" made of birch bark like a wigwam, but instead of using straight poles, the rolls of birch bark were spread over an elongated framework of poles, both ends of which were bent over and stuck in the ground forming a rounded building rather than an inverted cone shaped one.

Many of the treaty Natives here bore Scotch names such as MacDonald and Cameron and whether this denoted a mixed parentage in the remote past or whether some Scotch traders found it easier to give them these names rather than try to write their Native names is debatable, especially as some of the latter can be long as for instance "Muzzeneecootchegayinine" which was actually the name of a Native hunter at one of the posts and meant "Wood Carver" or actually "the man who carves patterns in wood."

There was an amusing tale concerning one of these Scotch Natives who was illiterate but pretended that he wasn't and subscribed to a newspaper "The Prairie Farmer" through the medium of the Post Manager, and which he'd receive through the mail by anyone going to town. He'd make a big show of being able to read it, for the benefit of other Natives. On one occasion, so the story goes, he had the paper upside down and, not realizing it, he proceeded to tell his listeners about some big steamship that had capsized. Actually, it was just some steamship company's advertisement that he was looking at upside down.

This old man lived near an outpost that we had at a lake called One Man's Lake, near the junction of the Winnipeg and English rivers and to which I'd make an occasional visit during winter, it being a day's journey by dog team.

In those days, a silver fox pelt was quite valuable, worth three hundred dollars, and black fox even more so, as much as eight hundred dollars. Now the art of dyeing red fox skins to imitate them (or maybe it is white fox I'm not sure) has reduced their value in the 1950's so that they were almost worthless and probably still are.

Well at this time, while I was at White Dog Post, it was known that somebody had trapped a silver fox, and immediate preparations were made to take a trip out at the old man's winter camp (usually a wigwam) and try to buy it before some other free trader got word of it and got out there first. Quite often such special trips would involve a day's journey or more each way and one was not always successful in getting the pelt. The Native, failing to appreciate any minor defects that detracted from its worth, would expect to get top price for what could well be far from top quality fur.

Also, during my stay there, some of the Natives were taken ill and it was found that they were suffering from typhoid, contracted, it was assumed, from drinking the river water, into which the city of Kenora discharged its sewage. As a result we were all instructed to boil our drinking water.

Many of the Natives had more confidence in their own medicine man, and it is doubtful if they complied with the doctor's instructions, however I do not recall that there were very many cases and, as I understood from the doctor whom I accompanied as interpreter, the disease was not contagious .

As I recollect, it was before the epidemic was over that we were transferred to Fort Hope Post, but before proceeding with that part of my narrative, I must record the birth of our first son on June 10, 1913, it being rather unusual.

On hearing that there was to be a big give away dance at Swan Lake or near there, to which Natives from all around (within a radius of possibly a hundred miles) would be attending, bedecked in all their finery of bead work, silk work and porcupine quills, we decided we'd take a tent and see them in spite of the fact that Eliza or Lisa as she preferred to be called was expecting in a matter of a month or so.

On arrival near the scene of the dance scheduled to start that evening, we pitched our tent and went for a paddle exploring some of the shores and bays. After our return to the tent where we made supper Lisa complained of not feeling well, so we called off the visit to the site of the dance. Later, though, she realized or thought that she was going into labor, so I had to leave her, hasten to the canoe and paddle for all I was worth to the scene of the dance. There, I was able to procure a midwife to accompany me back and sure enough within an hour or two she gave birth to our first son.

The next day, I secured help and we made a stretcher and brought my wife and my son, whom we named George, home. Lisa was none the worse, neither from the canoe ride home nor from the transportation to and from the canoe.

George was quite a big baby, between eight and nine pounds I believe, when weighed on the scoop of the store scales a day or two later. My big anxiety was that some of the well meaning Native women should endeavor to kiss him, knowing that Lisa thought it important to prevent such displays of affection and she tried to say this in as tactful a way as she could.

Chapter 18

North to Fort Hope – Eabametoong

Upon receiving word that we were to be moved to the Fort Hope Post, which was about three times as far from the railroad and as north-east away as I'd ever been, Lisa was not too happy. We had both enjoyed the White Dog Post but Lisa was a good woman and together we made the best of it. In July of 1914 we found ourselves heading out for a new place and were soon on our way.

This time we didn't have to go via Dinorwic, but via Sioux Lookout which was sometimes called the "Hub of the North" and was incorporated in 1912.

The name of Sioux Lookout came from a First Nation story about a nearby mountain. It seems that this mountain was used in the late 1700's by the local Ojibway Indians to watch out for Sioux warriors coming to ambush their camp. By carefully looking, a sharp-eyed Native could see the sun shining off the birch of the enemy canoes crossing nearby rapids. Then the women and children could be led away safely while the warriors could intercept the Sioux warriors in the water.

Sioux Lookout was near Hudson Bay, the railroad having been completed by then, and from there we followed the English River, skirting the end of Lac Seul and then we arrived at Root River, where we stopped to make lunch on the first portage. Here we encountered M.V.P.A. Godsell who was an author of a few books about the Hudson Bay Company and who was en route back from transporting some fur shipment destined I think to go out by the Company's ship from Albany.

At the time, Mr. Godsell was in a hurry to get back to civilization so it was just a case of hurried introductions and a speedy goodbye. This time we had a powerboat to take us to the Hudson Bay Company steam tug "Kay too" (named after the post number of K2), awaiting our arrival and on which we embarked with a long string of six or more canoes in tow behind us.

The weather was grand and we had to stop en route for a load of fuel consisting of wood from the adjacent bush. About halfway up the lake a stand of red pine was pointed out to me and I was told that those would be the last red pine I'd encounter from then on.

We arrived at the Osnaburgh post and found my old friend Jabez had been transferred and a Mr. Hooker had taken his place. We spent the night there and during our stay a Mr. Gordon, whose job I was taking over at Fort Hope, arrived. To my surprise, he thought he'd spend the day with me at the post.

He gave me instructions concerning the keeping of the meteorological records and the reading of the instruments consisting of maximum and minimum thermometers, also a wet bulb thermometer, a columnar barometer and a rain gauge with much of which I'd been unfamiliar; he also gave an illustrated instruction book on how to diagnose the clouds, wind velocities and more.

Apart from that there was not much he needed to tell me, that I couldn't learn from his Outpost Manager who during the summer months would be my chief assistant and adviser; and, a very great help he proved to be, especially in telling me when I should make provision for the making of snowshoes and toboggans in preparation for coming winters.

After spending the night at Osnaburgh we left the following morning in a "Lac Seul" freight canoe with a capacity of a ton and a half and a crew of five. I think we took about a ton of freight and baggage. The journey was to take us five days.

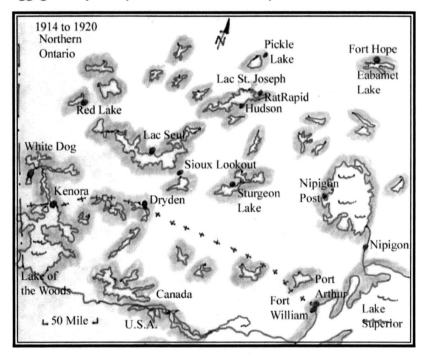

I must mention that, when leaving the railroad, I was given a clerk who accompanied us on the trip and who turned out to be a close friend of my cousin's over in England. The clerk's name was Pat Burbridge and the crew had some fun at his expense when we came to a very rough set of rapids they intended to run. This was not to be with us aboard, any doubt to lighten the load as well as to prevent us from getting a soaking from the spray. Pat however prevailed on the guide to let him stay aboard, so he accordingly assigned a place for him where he got a real sousing, or was it pure accident? I doubt it! Anyway he was the object of much friendly joking when we re-embarked at the foot of the rapids.

These Fort Hope Natives were the best canoe men in the district and were reputed to have run some rapids near Lac Seul or Hudson that the Lac Seul Natives always portaged around. Stops for lunch en route were very brief and the Natives would have baked their bannock and fried their salt bacon and be all ready to get going long before we were, but then of course Lisa had the one year old son to slow us down.

En route, we traveled through some burnt over country, the defoliated trees all black and some still smoldering and it was quite smoky. Here and there we'd see game, usually a rabbit or a red fox sitting on the shore having managed to escape the flames. In view of the nature of the country, which was largely interlaced with small stands of spruce, we concluded that it was not conductive to a raging type of fire especially with low winds.

Sometimes along the route we'd pull into some small stream where the Natives would catch a few brook trout, which was quite a treat, and of course pickerel and pike were available almost anywhere, but pike wasn't much good unless it was a good size of five or six pounds at the least.

Black flies and mosquitoes as well as sand flies all contributed to make life miserable and some mornings the outside of the tent was swarming with mosquitoes vainly endeavoring to get in, so great care was taken to pitch our tent in a manner that would leave no means of entry other than the door flap which of course admitted a few but these too were eliminated when we hung our mosquito bars at bedtime.

As we arrived at Eabamet Lake on a point where the post stands, we noticed that the bush fire we had encountered en route had now burnt through to a rocky point some two miles from the post, but as there appeared to be a big swamp intervening, I was not overly concerned.

Not so however with Sinclair who, greeting us on our arrival, expressed his feeling of relief at being relieved of the responsibility of taking what action he might think necessary on account of the fires. Well to me it seemed highly improbable that the buildings would be in any danger, situated as they were out on a long bare point and so I did nothing and it just smoldered away in the swamp until the first good rain came.

Eabametoong, which was also known as Fort Hope, was an Ojibway First Nation located in the Kenora District of northern Ontario. It was situated on the shore of Eabamet Lake in the Albany River system north of Beardmore, Ontario and was accessible only by water or traveling by icy river roads during the winter.

Eabametoong came to be during the fur trade era when the Hudson Bay Company set up a trading post by Eabamet Lake in 1890. As canoes were the main source of transportation the post had to be near water. The Fort Hope Band came into existence in 1905 when five hundred people signed a treaty. The name Eabametoong had a significant meaning in the Anishinnaabe language; it literally meant "the reversing of the water place".

The water flow from Eabamet Lake into the Albany River would reverse each year, such that the water flowed into Eabamet Lake from the Albany River for a short period of time.

Now I must tell of our arrival at the post where all the Natives were gathered around the dock to greet us which was something Lisa had hoped would not transpire. Apart from shaking hands with the Chief and Sinclair, however, we were not expected to go the rounds of the spectators and Sinclair took us over to the house.

What a house it was! It was all built of lumber and sawed with a whip saw, and then of course sanded down smooth with hand tools. The interior of the house was also all lined with six inch boards laid diagonally and planed to give the appearance of being built of three inch material and then all varnished. There was a hall running from the front door to the kitchen with doors on the side opening into the living room and the study. I thought this very unwise.

The building was two and a half stories high with a veranda upstairs and downstairs.

The upstairs veranda very nearly caused me to have a bad accident; one day, I was leaning out over the rail to see if some Native I'd sent home had really left or was still hanging around. The end of the rail, being half rotten, came loose and I just barely regained my balance as it swung out or I'd surely have landed head first.

The house was heated by a large collapsible iron box stove known as a Carron Stove, after the maker's name and which, if I remember correctly, was imported from England. There was also a wood burning range in the kitchen and these two stoves were all the heating facilities in the house, hence, my remarks about the hall being a mistake. Looking back and remembering how the stove pipes would get red hot and how with these pipes strung through unheated rooms upstairs, the condensation of the wood smoke would cause the stove pipe elbows to form that black liquid known as creosote.

Everything in the kitchen froze solid overnight including a cup of water containing my upper dentures which, not being noticed in the chunk of ice was thrown into the garbage and subsequently rescued from atop the frozen pile outside.

One of the first things to be thawed in the morning was our can of evaporated milk which was placed in the oven and on one occasion was overlooked. What a mess that made when it exploded!

Getting back to the day of our arrival and our first meal, we were all seated and starting to eat when, on looking up, there with their faces glued to the window were a crowd of Native children satisfying their curiosity. We resented being placed in the position of animals at a circus, so Pat enthusiastically welcomed the suggestion that he do what he could to discourage this practice. Just what he did or said I don't know, but the children lost no time in disappearing and never troubled us further.

Here the store was about a hundred feet or so away from the house and had an office in a separate room, each having separate entries. Both of these however were furnished with stoves, but which of course were never left burning all night and in consequence it took quite a while to get the buildings warmed up. Rather I should say that the books would freeze up and as a result it was some time before I realized that in spite of the use of blotting paper, my writing all became smudged to some extent. I finally realized that the books were so cold that the ink froze as soon as I wrote so the blotting paper had no effect and later when the pages warmed up the writing thawed and, being wet, the ink was easily smudged.

Eabamet Lake was just about on the height of land or just over it, so its waters drained into the Albany River and thence into the large body of water called James Bay. Whilst the winters were long and severe I do not recall that I ever recorded a minimum temperature of less than minus forty-five degrees Fahrenheit nor was the snowfall too great except during one of the six winters I was there.

We had two outposts there, the larger one being on Lansdowne Lake, but known to us at that time as Attawapiscat Lake. No doubt it was the headwaters of the river by the name of Lansdowne Lake or Attawapiscat Lake which emptied into the Hudson Bay. We also had another at Wabequai where Lisa's brother John was working.

Neither of these posts was kept open during the summer when the Natives of those localities moved in the Fort Hope area to participate in the job of freighting our supplies in by canoe, at that time from Hudson or Sioux Lookout.

Wabequai was reputed to be a wonderful spot for ducks and geese during their migrations and this actually was the incentive for John not wanting to be transferred elsewhere.

One day my clerk Pat, to whom such things as muzzle loading shot guns were a novelty, asked me the reason for an ornamental ring around the barrel some six inches or so from the nipple whereon the gun cap was placed. I jokingly remarked that it indicated the amount of load to be put in.

Some month or two later, when Pat was transferred to help John he bought a single band muzzle loading gun. Later John informed me that apparently he had taken my remark seriously regarding the loading and as a result the kick from the gun knocked him over and split the gun stock. Fortunately, he wasn't injured. At the time the joking remark was made, I certainly had no idea he planned on acquiring such a gun.

It was shortly after our arrival at Fort Hope that the Great War of 1914 broke out but we didn't hear of it until the last mail before freeze-up arrived. When we received our next mail in January I learned from my sister that two of my cousins with whom I'd gone to school with had joined up and gone to the front of the battle as well as an elder brother of theirs. As I'd mentioned earlier they were both tragically killed in action.

In 1915, when the treaty party arrived to pay the Natives their annual treaty money of four dollars per head, the treaty paymaster also endeavored to recruit Natives for the army, but as I recollect he only got two. Had it not been for my two year old son I'd have gone as well as it would have afforded me the opportunity of visiting my sister in England.

I was however not prepared to have my son under the jurisdiction of my in-laws, and so I gave up the opportunity of joining the Forestry Corps for whom the paymaster was recruiting and whose services were mainly if not totally occupied in Scotland.

There was an opposition post of Réveillon Frères, a short distance from our store. This post was under the management of Jack Spence and I decided not to let our business competition interfere with our own personal feelings and as a result we became good friends and we'd often go hunting together in a canoe.

Jack told me of an amusing episode regarding my predecessor who, having shot a duck and only wounding it, wrung its neck and threw it behind him in the canoe; but, shortly after, he heard a commotion behind him and turned around just in time to see his duck take off. Apparently it had only been stunned and he'd made a poor job of wringing its neck.

There were two churches at Fort Hope, the Anglican Church being just across the creek from the Hudson Bay Company and the Roman Catholic Church near the post of Réveillon Frères. The Anglican Church was under Reverend Richards, a brother of the old gentleman working in the store at Osnaburgh. He was married and had a family of four or five as I recollect and, having at one time been stationed at Great Whale River, which I think was at Rupert's House, was able to tell us some very interesting stories about the life up there and the white foxes that were so very abundant during his stay.

The Roman Catholic church however was a Jesuit Mission and was only served by the priest two or three times a year, notably at Christmas when he was the recipient of a fair quantity of furs donated by his members in lieu of cash and at treaty time when the Natives got their four dollars per head.

We used to estimate that of all the Natives one third were Roman Catholic, one third Anglican and one third pagan, so called. It was said that the pagans rated first in so far as honesty in paying their bills, and the Roman Catholics, last. One of these pagan Natives who was not honest, however, came to see me in the office and told me about his beliefs, which included re-incarnation. He said he would be reborn seven times, so I told him he'd better be sure and pay his bills and be honest, as this might well be his seventh life, to which he replied, "No, this is only the fifth one," with such complete assurance.

After the Natives had all left for their trapping grounds, I had a trap line of my own and the first year I caught some minks only to find out that, as a result of the war, the bottom had fallen out of the fur market, and these animals' furs were only worth from fifty cents to seventy-five cents apiece. Rather than let them go for so little I gave them to my wife, asking her to make them up into a pair of fur lined gauntlet mitts, which she did. Next year the prices were back up around six or seven dollars so I was sorry I hadn't held them over, but they'd probably have gotten wormy during the summer heat anyway.

On one of my longer trips entailing an all day hike, I used to take one of my Native helpers named John Gordevin and I would usually carry a compass, but, on one occasion, I forgot to do so. John suggested we take a shortcut and, the day being cloudy and snowing, I left it to him to break trail, and after walking an hour or so we hit fresh snowshoe tracks, but John recognized them as being our own, so I realized that we were lost. John then undertook to climb a tree and he'd point in the direction we should go and I'd take note of it by making a mark in the snow.

So, we started out again and it wasn't long until we hit our own trail again so I told John that whilst I didn't pretend to know as much about the bush as he, I didn't propose to follow him around in circles all day. I therefore waited and let him go ahead as far as I could watch him and noted that he appeared to be gradually veering to the left. I quit his trail and swung off more to the right and sure enough came to a rocky hill whereupon I started to holler for John.

Meantime, I made a fire, remembering that he was carrying the tea kettle. Now that we'd crossed the large swamp where every small spruce tree looked like the next, John had no difficulty in finding the trail we'd been looking for, and he led us back to the post.

I guess these Natives and Métis who work at the posts did not have the experience to make them good bush men. I was told that another one who worked for Jack Spence was met on the trail late in the day and, being asked where he was going, said he'd been out hunting and was on his way home. It was remarked to him that he was going in the opposite direction to where he should be going. This of course can easily happen if one hits a trail running crossway to the direction one's headed for and if the sky is overcast.

Once, when we were getting some logs cut along the lakeshore, we had four or five Natives cutting and hewing. Hewing is a method of cutting wood for the purpose of dressing a timber to the desired form or shape. Historically it was a method of squaring-up beams for construction. It was very labor intensive, so we would only square one surface, or around the area that was necessary to make the joints.

That day, during his lunch break, one of the Natives stuck his butcher knife into one of the logs that was being cut and he forgot to pull it out with the result that, when the log was being pulled down to the shore, the blade of the knife caught one chap in the calf of his legs, leaving an awful gash right to the bone, I believe.

Not having much, if any, knowledge of how to treat such severe wounds, I was glad to avail myself of the services of the Jesuit Priest who had just arrived for the treaty and he poured iodine into the wound and bound it up. Fortunately the treaty party arrived the next day with a doctor who always accompanied them and he sewed up the wound, giving me instructions to pull the stitches out five days later, explaining to me how I should do it, and thank goodness I had no problems with the wound to contend with. There were numerous accidents during my tenure in office in which, no doctor being available, the Natives treated the wounds themselves.

There was the occasion when one Native who lived some fifty miles or more away from the post just about blew his hand to pieces with the blast from a rifle or shotgun. I heard about it but didn't see him until some weeks later when his hand was all bound up with rags and rabbit skins, it being winter. I suggested to his relatives that he should be taken out to see a doctor, but he didn't do so until the following summer by which time it had healed without apparently any infection setting in.

One day, Lisa and I were out trolling in the canoe some miles from home when the troll got caught in some weeds. I was sitting in the bow and gave a tug on the line just as Lisa put her hand in the water to see if she could disentangle it and, as a result, it pulled off with a jerk and hooked her finger right over the barb. She was all for leaving it until we got home, but, remembering it was an old rusty troll, I wouldn't hear of it so I took my pocket knife, which I was able to sharpen on a smooth rock, and made a quick gash in her finger.

We had a Native woman with us and she promptly cut some bark off a willow of some kind, chewed it up and applied it as a poultice; as a result, no infection set in and it healed without any trouble.

Every spring and fall we used to go out camping for a few weeks. In the spring we'd take our tent and necessities on a dog sleigh to a narrows where the lake entered into the river which was the first part to open, and there, we'd spend the time fishing along with duck and goose hunting.

One spring, the first I think (as George was wearing a skirt and couldn't have been more than two years old), as we were paddling home with our canoe loaded with our belongings, Lisa in the bow, George fell overboard. I was in the stern and I reached down, grabbed his skirt as he was going down and fished him out of the ice cold water. After going ashore and getting some dry warmed-up clothes on him he was none the worse, but what a fright that was!

A few years later, when we went out duck hunting and stopped for lunch, I stood my loaded gun against a tree at what I thought was a safe distance away, but George was at the age when he could get around fast and, whilst we were otherwise engaged washing out the dishes down on the shore, there was a sudden bang and it seemed George had toddled over to the gun and pulled the trigger and, it being a hammer-type gun without any safety catch, it went off with a loud roar. Fortunately he hadn't knocked it down so the discharge went straight up.

In September, 1914 our second son Walter was born, and our first daughter Lorna in March, 1917 so Lisa had her hands full with three young children. We decided to hire a Native woman to help us and who accompanied us on our camping out excursions.

One spring, in the month of April, having heard that there was a large number of prairie chickens at a small lake some eight or ten miles away, and it being their mating season when they engaged in a dance ritual, we decided we'd like to see it. Since they did their dance early in the morning, we left the day previous with our tent and sleeping bags, and enough grub for a couple of meals.

The weather, however, turned unusually mild. The slight frost during the night produced a light crust on the snow that was strong enough to support us on snowshoes in some places only, making the snowshoeing from our camp to the place where the prairie chickens performed their dance pretty tough going.

On the way to that site, we could hear foxes barking not too far away and presumed they'd been preying on the birds as none showed up for their dance, although their tracks were visible in places. By the time we reluctantly gave up our watch for them and got back to our tent, the weather had gotten so warm that the lakes were covered with water, so we decided to spend the day there, and have another hunt for the dancing birds early the next morning, but alas, we saw nothing of them and had to return home, the weather having turned really cold again. Traveling with Lisa, however, had made it a fun excursion.

Chapter 19

Spanish Flu, Appendicitis & the HBC 250th Anniversary

It was whilst I was at Fort Hope that the big Spanish Flu epidemic took place, but we were fortunate and the epidemic seemed to have missed us entirely. We had no reports of any Natives in the vicinity of our post or any other outposts nearby suffering from that deadly flu bug.

Not so however at Savant Lake where there were so many deaths that the bodies were placed in a building there and cremated, nobody being strong enough to chop out the frozen ground for their internments. One of my outside workers John (who accompanied me the time we got lost) succumbed to the flu when he went out to the line to get the mail, and was buried at Fort William, I think.

That fall, the lake being frozen without any snow, I skated around to see some fox traps I'd set and, on my return home, took quite seriously ill, so it was decided to send a couple of men out with a letter to the District Office in Fort William describing my symptoms to get a diagnosis.

As it was late in the fall, the Natives had a hard time owing to some lakes being still open and others frozen, so their journey out took considerable time. Meantime, I recuperated to the extent that

I was sufficiently recovered to refrain from taking the medicine they brought with them and which in spite of their care had been frozen and would not mix when shaken.

The year 1919 came and Lisa gave birth to our third son, christened John Anthony, whom we named after a distant predecessor by the name of Anthony Deane. My intention was to call him John but Tony he became.

The following summer, however, with what appeared to be similar symptoms coming on, I went out at the line to see a doctor who said I must have suffered an attack of acute appendicitis from which I fortunately recovered and was now suffering from chronic appendicitis. On his advice I had an operation which in those days required a stay of ten days in the hospital, seven at which were spent in bed.

The day I was discharged from the Prince of Wales Hospital I heard that a big event was taking place outside. I went directly to the Station to join the throng. There was an airplane in operation taking people for joy rides for, I believe, fifteen dollars for fifteen minutes. I gazed with wonder at the airplane. However, I didn't end up going for a ride.

Whilst my stitches had not healed entirely, following a problem with them in the hospital, my doctor did consider it safe for me to return to my post provided I did no lifting. I left the following day in the company of a new clerk who had just returned from the war and had been a lieutenant overseas.

Later that fall, I was out hunting birds with Jack Spence and, on stopping to light a fire at lunch time, felt some pain where I'd had my incision for the appendicitis; on looking to see, I noticed a swelling there which rather disconcerted me. I got Lisa to make me a pad and bandage and wore that all the time until some months later when I could get out to see my doctor who diagnosed it as a stitch ulcer that had not been properly attended to; and, after swabbing out the now open sore, assured me it should give me no further trouble, so I returned to my post.

The following spring was 1920 and it was the two hundred and fiftieth anniversary of the Hudson Bay Company. We were instructed to put on a feast for the Natives on the auspicious day of the second of May which we did to the best of our ability out in the open, the weather fortunately being favorable.

At that time of the year, as freighting had not commenced, our supplies were at a low point, but such items as stewed prunes, rice and apple sauce with raisin bannock were to some of them no doubt a luxury. There were a few complaints that some were getting prunes and others were not, so it had to be explained to them that they would be getting apple sauce instead and that this was as much a treat as the other items.

Alas I never was one for making long explanations so I left it to my able assistant Sinclair who could also speak more fluently than I could in their Native language.

During the first year we were at Fort Hope, a red deer was seen up the river and I was told it was the first one seen anywhere around that part of the country.

At Fort Hope, I was also instrumental in introducing fox snaring which was the only method adopted at the White Dog Post, but it was scoffed at when I first mentioned it to Sinclair until it proved to be indeed practical.

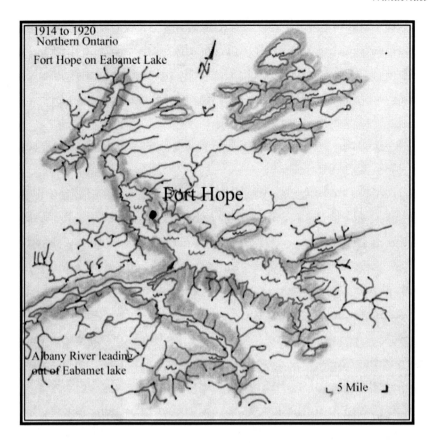

The cost of bringing in supplies was high, as much as ten dollars per measure, which made the price of flour prohibitive to the poorer trappers, so we actually sold our flour at less than cost. We did however recover the loss entailed by charging what the uninformed would consider excessive prices on such luxury articles as silk handkerchiefs or head squares and other unnecessary items, thus enabling the poor hunter to buy at least a modicum of flour. Instead of sugar we sold saccharine to the Natives who were fond of sweetening their food and could carry their requirements in their pockets.

During my stay at Fort Hope I had occasion to visit our chief outpost at Attawapiscat Lake known as Lansdowne House which surpassed our Fort Hope Post in importance. During one trip there I was told that one small lake we crossed was known as Muchoochahn Lake and that meant Hot Bath Lake, the Natives at one time having a wigwam with a pole of rocks that they heated up and then poured water on, much as the Finlanders must have done in their primitive saunas.

I never did get out to Wabiquai which was, I think, some three days journey further on.

It might be of interest here to mention that, in addition to our outposts, we also had camp trades at Snake Falls on the Albany River and at Beaver Lodge. These just constituted supplies of dry food goods and ammunition given out to certain Natives of good repute to trade with for furs from Natives camped in their localities.

Correspondence with these camp traders was done in syllables as well as picture writing by drawing pictures of objects required. Sometimes errors were made as for instance when my trader ordered some rolls of snuff and I misread it as ribbon, the Native word for which is similar to the English word for snuff, which they used. It's not hard to imagine the indignation such an error would cause especially if the trader was a heavy user of snuff.

Chapter 20

Longlac, Ontario

In 1920, on going to town for what I thought was to be our vacation, I learned that we wouldn't be going back to Fort Hope as we were to be transferred to Longlac, where our children would be closer to schools.

When we arrived at the track Lisa went on a trip to Minaki to visit her parents, taking the children with her, whilst I went east to Fort William where the District Office was located. It was not in its original setting above the Hudson Bay Company store which had burnt down in 1914, but in a building on May Street. It was not until my arrival there that I was informed of my transfer.

Jack Spence of the Réveillon Frères Post at Fort Hope had been at Longlac prior to going to Fort Hope and, from what he'd told me of the Natives there, I can't say that I looked forward to the change.

After a brief holiday, I left for Longlac on the local, a freight train with one passenger coach at the end. The one hundred and eighty mile trip took the best part of a day, what with all the train's stops and shunting, as well as waiting for a half hour or more on some siding to let another freight train pass.

On arrival at the station consisting of what appeared to be a converted box car, I made enquiries to the station mistress, who turned out to be a lady by the name of Haynes, as to the location of the post where I would be working. It turned out that it was some two miles or so across the bay and she said the Native in temporary charge there would probably be over later to pick up the mail.

I decided to seat myself on a pile of ties and await his arrival as the weather was nice, although the flies were bad. In due course Nichol Finlayson came across in a canoe and took me across to the post. The house I'd visited back in 1906 had been replaced, but there stood the fine log store, the completion of which I'd witnessed. An addition had been made, though, in the form of a small log office building. It had been probably constructed from the logs of the old replaced house. There were no longer any cattle although the old milk house was still there.

The post was quite a picturesque spot, situated in a cove on a rocky point with a background of some hundred acres of cleared land and the Roman Catholic Church some hundred yards or so away.

The steamboat that had been in use freighting supplies was no longer there, having been sunk in a bay down near the narrows where it had been left unattended during a winter, developing a leak and sinking, so I was told. There was however a motor launch with an inboard four cylinder engine that had formerly been down at Nipigon but, owing to its narrow beam in proportion to its length, was considered unsafe for the rapid waters down there and was now in use for freighting supplies from the railroad.

Nichol Finlayson turned out to be a man in his seventies who had been temporarily in charge of the post in Longlac. He had an adopted boy named Willie White around the age of sixteen who helped him out a good deal.

A week or so after my arrival, I had to go to Minaki to pick up my family who had all been down with the measles and were still looking very pale. As the railroad cut off from Longlac we came in by canoe from Cavell where there was a small village of Natives near the banks.

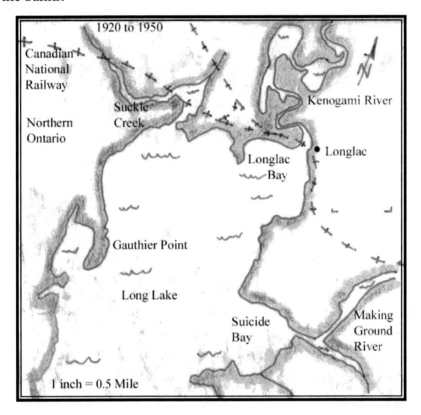

The Company had a boxcar station near the railroad. Near there were also three railroad section houses and two stores, one owned and operated by Gean Mathe and the other owned by a small company known I think as the Great Lakes Trading Company, which was operated by Emile Finlayson, who turned out to be a son of Nichol. We stayed there for the day.

Gean Mathe also catered to tourists and, shortly after our arrival, our son George came down with pneumonia. We didn't realize how serious his illness was, but Lisa had him all bundled up in numerous blankets as he was shivering. Gean Mathe on hearing about it brought over one of his tourists, a man named St Manion who had kindly volunteered his services free before leaving on his moose hunting trip.

The first thing he did was to open a window and remove the heavy blanket for, as he said, George had all the cold he'd be able to catch. He then instructed Lisa to bathe him with tepid water if his fever was running high and to give him a teaspoon of brandy two or three times a day. Anyway, after carefully following his instructions, we were able to restore him to good health, but how fortunate we were to have the doctor, who later became quite a celebrity or at any rate a popular figure.

During the winter I was awakened one night by Nick Finlayson my assistant who said some Natives had arrived from Heron Bay on the north shore of Lake Superior with a quantity of beaver pelts. He said one of these men was wanted on suspicion of murder and one as being an accessory, which was why they had made the long trip up rather than trying to sell them at nearer stores along the Canadian Pacific Railway.

Well, I must say, it was with some trepidation that I got up and opened the store, the more so because in those days we used to sell a supposedly non-intoxicating beer to the Natives. They would drink a lot of it, mixing snuff or chewing snuff at the same time, and thereby getting in a state of mild intoxication, or they sometimes added other ingredients which would get them really drunk. Fortunately, they were in a hurry to finish their transactions and get away without wasting any more time than necessary.

During the winter I also had occasion to make a snowshoe trip to McKay Lake some twenty miles or more as I recollect, and we spent the night in a Native's tent, wigwams becoming obsolete by then. It was quite a large tent as his family consisted of five people, although as I recollect only three were home at the time. This family proved to be full of tuberculosis which carried most of them away in their prime; however, I must admit that in all my years of trading with the Natives the chance of contracting it never occurred to me. I guess I saved myself a lot of needless worry in that respect.

On arrival home from this trip, I discovered that my appendix incision had partially re-opened, necessitating another trip to my doctor who repeated his last technique of swabbing it out and this time, fortunately, for my peace of mind, it stayed healed.

At this post, we'd acquired a small long haired dog we called Wargush which meant "fox" in the Native language. This poor dog unfortunately followed one of Nick's snare trails in the bush and was strangled in one of the snares. This was the story that we were told, although we found it hard to believe that a rabbit snare would hold him.

This first winter at Longlac proved to be an eventful one. One of our log buildings near the store was what was known as the Native house and was utilized solely by Natives arriving by train late at night. They would walk the two miles across to the post and proceed to fire up the stove there without disturbing anybody.

On one occasion when the Inspector was visiting our spot and spending the night with us, there was a knocking at the door, and an excited Native said "boarding house burning" and I presumed he referred to the old boarding house at the railroad. As I looked out the window in another one of the other rooms I discovered it was our Native house which was already a mass of flames. There was nothing we could do to save it. Fortunately, the four or five Natives managed to escape unharmed. They lost all their furs and it became evident they had been drinking, no doubt procuring it from some bootleggers or even a railroad man who might have wanted to get a skin or two from them.

During the fall of 1920 the lake had frozen sufficiently for travel. We had a heavy snowfall followed by a big thaw that left the lake appearing like open water and I found it rather an eerie experience riding across to the station on a dog sleigh with no means of discerning any weak spots on the ice. I expect there was actually little danger at the time; however, we did hear that the Chief of the band at Cavell, traveling under the same conditions, had disappeared under the ice with his dogs and sleigh and all drowned! What a tragedy!

The treaty payment which fell early in the summer of 1921 became the scene of water sports events, consisting of canoe racing of various kinds, some with one paddler only seated in the bow, others with men competing with women and ending up with a tug of war on land.

Later in the summer we had to get started on moving the post across the bay to a site right behind the station. As the store was made of logs, I first of all I took a paint brush and numbered each log from the bottom up, so that there would be no problem in reassembling them in the same manner. It was suggested that I'd have difficulty with the tapered and burled key that kept the logs from spreading, but I experienced none as, by using a crowbar, one only had to pry them up a foot or so and they fell right out.

Large rafts were then made of the logs, and the windows, door frames and shelving were all piled onto them and towed across to the shore from where they were hauled to the new site.

The residence house however was not moved and a new one was being built for us. We did move one of the servant's log houses for the clerk's family. With the old store building still left at the old site, we continued to carry on business until such a time as the log warehouse had been completed. We utilized that as a makeshift store, using empty cases piled sideways on each other to form shelves, but actually when it came down to it we were only closed for one day.

As our new house had not yet been completed, we stayed in a large tent for a short time, then into a small building that was subsequently to become a Native American house.

Meantime, the reconstruction of the old store was being carried out by some Natives from the Lac Seul area by our new District Manager J.D. McKenzie who had formerly been in charge of the Lac Seul post for many years. His father had also been a District Manager there as had his grandfather. The Natives may have been some of his boyhood friends, and the fact that they were good carpenters afforded a good excuse for giving them this job. This no doubt was performed at a big saving to what it otherwise would have cost.

In view of the size of my family, now consisting of four children, making six of us in all, it was decided we should get a cow and so we bought a fine large Durham one as well as a horse to haul our wood of which we'd burn close to forty cords of four inch wood per winter.

Nick Finlayson had now been pensioned off and his eldest son, Emile, was running the opposition fur trading post next to us. My new helper was a distant relation of Nick's by the name of Ben Finlayson who, with a wife and two sons, moved into the servants' house that had been moved.

The area fronting the store and dwelling wasn't very attractive, consisting as it was of a sea of old log stumps which, as I recollect, remained for a few years until sufficiently rotted to make their demolition easy.

There was good speckled trout fishing some four miles away, not to mention pickerel at the river bridge. I'd never done any angling since I'd come to Canada and as I sat in my office, a Mexican or part Mexican chap who went by the name of Charlie Bunby, (but whose real name was reported to me as being Philip Andrada) ,whose job was patrolling the railroad on a speeder for the Forestry, dropped in one day, trying to coax me to take some time off.

Well, he got his fishing rod and showed it along with another one he kept as an extra. He convinced me that we could take his speeder to a branch of Rocky Shore Creek which passed under the railroad some four miles east, and that I could try my hand at speckled trout fishing.

During my years of work I was always too busy but, one day, I weakened and, after that, you couldn't keep me away from fishing at "95" every fine Sunday during the summer months, or taking a half day off to do so when business was slack. Sometimes I'd borrow a speeder from the pump man at the train station.

On one occasion I took a man named Crawford, who was a traveler for Imperial Tobacco Company, along and on our way home he looked around and saw behind us a train only a pole's length away, which was the distance between two telegraph poles. Crawford jumped off and I endeavored to throw myself and the speeder off but only proceeded in throwing myself which was perhaps better for me. The speeder continued on its way and was shortly struck amidships and only suffered the breakage of the cross-bar extending out to the single wheel.

When no means of transport were available, I'd quite often walk, getting up at an early hour on some Sundays, and I would arrive at the creek around seven a.m. in time for early morning fishing. At other times, I'd take the motor launch and go down river to the first set of rapids, where there was also good trout fishing.

One late Easter, Lisa and I went canoeing down the river. Noticing a dead tree lying halfway across the river partly submerged with a few branches sticking up, I remarked to Lisa that one of them looked just like a goose; and, that was just what it turned out to be. I grabbed my gun and as the goose came out of the water, I was able to shoot it.

Alas, one is not allowed to shoot geese in the spring and so, en route home, we gave it to some Natives we met, asking them to bring it over to the store later, as the Natives were allowed some privileges not accorded to the white man. Their treaty rights included unhindered hunting and trapping rights. That incidentally was the one and only goose I ever shot.

Shortly after we moved the store, the railroad put in a new concrete bridge to replace the long wooden trestle that was in use. The top sections of the bridge were made on the bank bordering the lake just in front of our store and I found it quite interesting to walk down and watch the progress from the metal reinforcement to the finished tops.

At the time the store was moved, there had been much speculation as to where the railroad would be built. The new station, in connection with the planned cut off to the town of Nakina, was the reason the store had not been moved earlier. We actually took a gamble in choosing the site we did. It proved to be a bad one as, to everybody's surprise, the new station was built at what was its present site until 1970. We were left with siding and a flag stop known as Calong, our former boxcars' station being removed and replaced by a small freight shed of similar proportions. The building of the train railway cut off in 1923 afforded considerable interest to me, although it was some two miles or so from the post.

In 1922 on March 6, Lisa gave birth to our second daughter whom we named Florence after my sister but Mildred soon became her name after a distant cousin of mine. Whilst it was my intention to call her by her first name, her second name became the one she was known by just as in the case of Tony, whom I'd planned calling John, as well as my second son, who was also known by his second name.

It must have been around this time that arrangements were made between Gean Mathe and me for the holding of school classes in a small log building behind our store under the tutelage of a Mrs. MacManus. Not long after, a man was needed to do the outside chores. I hired my friend Ownby and the log shack became his residence whilst school became properly established in a little Red School house behind Mathe's store.

One day, whilst I was in the stable milking the cow, someone came running in to tell me that Mildred had fallen off the dock into deep water; fortunately she had been fished out in time by one of the Natives encamped nearby and she was none the worse for her dunking.

A year or two after we moved the post, somebody fishing the creek at "95", neglected to put out their fire and as a result started a bush fire of considerable size, but whilst some of us were wondering if we'd have to vacate, what with intervening swamps and a timely rainfall, we were fortunately saved from having to do so. Also, it must have been about this time that the first Forestry Branch was established at Longlac, and their efforts at combating the fire must have been a factor in saving the settlement.

What must have been the first public entertainment was a picnic for the Canadian National Railway employees of the Hornepayne division consisting of sports, both water and land. It was put on at Picnic Point and was open to all residents. The only water sports I recollect were some wash tub races, for which a dozen or two galvanized wash tubs had been brought in. These were all brand new and, nobody apparently having been appointed to ensure their return, the wash tubs were for the most part missing the next morning, the Natives being suspected of having helped themselves to them.

The weather was perfect as I remember it and everybody seemed to have enjoyed themselves; however, the project was never repeated owing to the theft of supplies.

When I arrived in 1920 there were a few Native houses on the point of the Longlac band, but now they were increasing and the Roman Catholics proceeded to build a new church there; it was quite an improvement from the old log building!

In August of 1924, we had another addition to our family, a third daughter whom I named Edith Vera, Edith being the name of a sister who predeceased me in my infancy, and a name I always liked, as well as Vera, named after one of my first cousins.

In those days, nobody was worrying about the population explosion and in 1926 we had our seventh child, a daughter whom we named Ethel Ruth after nobody in particular, but both names of which I was particularly fond of.

Lorna by this time was getting old enough to help her mother and do her share of the household chores and the newly arrived additions to our family. Thinking back, it must have imposed a lot of work on her and deprived her of many playtime hours.

It must have been in 1928 that George, now fifteen, was offered a job with the Hudson Bay Company and duly left for Grand Lake Victoria in Québec with my prayers for his welfare and a long letter of fatherly advice from which I hope he reaped some benefit. He was back home again, however, in a couple of years or so and was then given charge of the Cavell post until it burnt down a year or two later.

Walter, meantime, had been given a job with the Hudson Bay Company at Kekkeingizami Outpost, later being transferred to Dinorwic post where he clerked for a few months before taking up prospecting and marrying Loretta Gascon by whom he had two children, a daughter whom they named Shirley and a son born a year or so prior to his death when he fell from a moving passenger train, and whom they also named Walter.

About this time, I think it was, that Lorna went to Oba to work for a Mrs. Hapbliss as a nursemaid for her children, and as sorry as I was to see her go, I was glad for her sake as I figured she'd be in a good Christian home; but, our home was never the same after she left, as I knew would inevitably be the case.

It also must have been around this time that the Little Red School house was burnt down and for a time classes had to be held in a railroad car parked on a siding.

Chapter 21

Oh, how the years go by!

About this time I was taken ill and had to leave for the hospital in Hornepayne just as the German plane the Dornur Wahl, captained by Herr Von Groneau, landed to take on some Shell Gas which was stored in our care. As my train pulled in just as he came ashore, my conversation with him was brief.

Dr. Dollars of Hornepayne was my doctor and in those days prescriptions or interviews were a dollar so his name was as appropriate as that of the minister who was Rev. Heaven.

Anyway, I wasn't there long before being transferred to the care of Dr. McKellip of Nakina who diagnosed the problem I was having in the calf of my leg. This kept me in bed for two weeks, after he explained to me the danger of the blood clot moving to the heart or brain. On looking back I can't help but think that he exaggerated the risk of such a thing happening.

During my hospitalization, Lorna left for Fort William to attend high school there, but for some reason the school was late in opening, so Walter, who was up there on business, dropped in to see her and persuaded her to accompany him home.

It must have been in 1937 that the bush fires were very bad all around us. It was also the start of the gold rush up the Suicide River.

One day, a customer dropped in telling me of an outcropping of gold bearing quartz that he'd found up there. After staking some claims, he'd left a mark on the river bank in case I wanted to go and stake some too. So, after telling some friends, they decided to take a run up there that same evening if I'd accompany them. After the store closed, I went along with them although it was dusk and we camped at the portage leaving at daybreak for our destination, which we found without too much trouble, and proceeded to stake out our quota of claims, being allowed nine claims of forty acres if I remember right, or three for each of us.

Unfortunately the veins ran into the Native reserve property where mining regulations were pretty strict, but we did get somebody to take an option on our claims that netted us some two hundred dollars apiece, which wasn't too bad for a day's work.

Our claims were not far from the Theresa Gold Mine which got as far as setting up a stamp mill and pouring one gold brick before folding up. Longlac became the scene of a gold rush following the discovery of the Little Longlac Mine at what is now the town of Geraldton, but at that time it was just bush land.

One evening, there was a knock on our door and a stranger by the name of Alec Gemmell, accompanied by his son Jack and two other lads I think, stated they had just arrived on the train from Toronto on a prospecting trip and were hockey fans, and asked if they could listen to the Stanley Cup final hockey game on our radio. We struck up an acquaintance with the family; one member whose name was Jack was eventually destined to become a son-in-law, when in 1939 he married our daughter Lorna. Lucky Jack and Lorna, I always liked him from the beginning.

In 1937 I was suffering from a bad case of ulcers which necessitated my going to Toronto to the Lockwood Clinic on Bloor Street for a diagnosis of my trouble. I was informed that I needed an operation and it would have to be there because the facilities were not available at the Lakehead Hospital in the Fort William and Port Arthur area. I was hospitalized for some ten days.

On my return, I was rather surprised to find nobody at the train station to meet me, until I heard that they were all quarantined owing to Edith having come down with an attack of polio and having been flown to the hospital at Lakehead. So, for a week or two I had to stay in the clerk's house with Lisa, she having been away from home at the time the quarantine was put on. Fortunately Edith's polio affected her leg only, leaving one leg an inch or two shorter than the other.

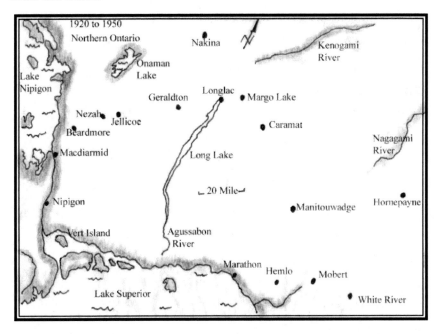

It must have been the following year that Tony enlisted in the Canadian Forestry Corps which was an administrative corps of the Canadian army; he was, I believe, the first resident of Longlac to do so. During his stay in Scotland, he was able to visit my sister in Somerset, England.

The Forestry Corps was created during the First World War when it was discovered that huge quantities of wood were needed for use on the Western Front. Duckboards, shoring timbers, crates, anything that needed wood had to be provided for. The British Government decided that there was no one more qualified in the British Empire to harvest timber than the Canadians.

At first, the idea was to harvest trees from Canada's abundant forests and bring them overseas. But this idea wasn't practical with space on board merchant ships at a premium; so, rather than stuff the ships' holds with timber, it was decided that Canadians be brought over to Europe to cut down forests in the United Kingdom and in France. Some regiments, originally slated for the front lines, became military lumberjacks' units instead and the Canadian troops, with their coniferous tree badges, identified them as the Canadian Forestry Corps cutting trees in England, Scotland and France, where the timber was squared, sawed and transported.

They had many assignments which even took them to the front lines, building aerodromes in France for the ever-growing Royal Flying Corps. Altogether, some thirty-five thousand Canadians served in the Forestry Corps and, while only some saw them as soldiers fighting behind the lines, they were an important part of the war and many died.

Also, about this time, Mildred left for Port Arthur to attend Business College and she stayed there for about ten months, following which she was able to find a job at Chapple's Department store in Geraldton. A year or so after Tony's enlistment, Lorna and Jack were married, the Rev. Bradbury of Hornepayne officiating. It must have been the following year, I think, that I paid them a visit to their home in Noranda, where Jack was working for a mining company, The Waite Amulet Mine. Their first son "Sandy" was less than a year old.

A year or so later, the Company decided to build us a new dwelling house, but nothing was said to me concerning it, so when the contractors arrived stating their mission, I said there must be some mistake as I had no knowledge that the Company had any such building in mind and that it was a new store rather than a dwelling that we needed.

However, they assured me there was no mistake and, a few months later, we moved into a four bedroom home with electric lighting furnished by a small Delco generator in the basement, a hot water tank heated from the kitchen range and more. These were all luxuries to which we had not been accustomed, and the gasoline washing machine must have proved a godsend to Lisa, although it was quite frequently a nuisance to me when it refused to start. Most often my services were requested usually when I could not spare the time from work but which I did find somehow.

Our Delco generator also created problems for one as ignorant of electrical matters as I was. Once, a brilliant flash occurred as I turned a switch on for some electrical item, and this caused me to beat a hasty retreat. I discovered later that it was caused by a loose battery connection, causing an arc which burnt the connecting post off the battery.

On another occasion, a lad ,who I had helping whilst I was busy in the store, undertook to fill the small tank carrying down some three gallons of gasoline in a large open tapped coffee pot such as were used in camps. Slipping on the stairs he fell, spilling all the contents on the basement floor, there being a fire on in the furnace at the time. A call for help from the house had me dashing over there and yelling for an immediate evacuation of the house by all the inhabitants including the lad whom I found feverishly engaged in mopping up the gas before it got near the furnace, he not realizing the danger of the fumes causing an explosion which fortunately didn't occur.

It must have been in 1942 that George enlisted in the Air Force and was stationed at Dorval, Québec until his health necessitated his retirement following attacks of ulcers which by now I felt ran in our family. Then, in 1943, he married Myrette Le Gallain in Montréal on April first, and was at that time employed with a ship building firm, subsequently moving to Port Arthur a few years later.

During all these years the settlement at Longlac had continued to grow and gone were many of the attractive scenes of nature, to be replaced by lumber camps. The lake became more hazardous with floating logs and dead heads, and the fishing creeks were denuded by the influx of anglers from Geraldton.

However, when Lorna and Jack visited us with their three youngsters a few years later, Jack was able to bring home a fine catch of speckled trout from the Suicide River, but drew a blank at Lukinto Lake where I accompanied him. We spent the day trying the devise methods of hooking some of the fine specimens of speckled trout that could be seen swimming around lazily on the bottom in some ten or fifteen feet of water; but, they refused to so much as take notice of our bait, which consisted of flies and juicy worms.

Yes, fishing can sure be frustrating at times, but we enjoyed the outing.

About this time, the new Anglican church was nearing completion, a project in which I'd taken an active part in the fundraising campaign, and Lorna, expressing her desire to have some small part in the project, accompanied me over and nailed a board on the building.

I had for a year or so held Sunday school in the new school house and was subsequently appointed SS. Superintendent of the new church, a post which I held for some two years. I was also the warden owing to our proximity to the church, but I had no bell to toll. I had many other jobs to do, though, such as filling the gasoline lamps, pumping them up to light and hanging them in their appointed places, and, in winter, there was that big camp heater stove to fire up and stoke with logs well ahead of service time.

All of this gave me a feeling of satisfaction that at least I was playing some small part in keeping up the cause of Christianity.

Our church, whilst originally built under the suggestion of Bishop Walton who at that time was the Rector of the Anglican Church in Geraldton, was subsequently to become an inter-denominational church, there not being sufficient Anglicans to finance the project in Longlac at that time. Certain members of other denominations wouldn't contribute to an Anglican Church, but were willing to do so if it were an inter-denominational one.

As the population of the village continued to grow and the completion of the highway made it more accessible, the need for a jail and local constables became apparent and the break and entering of our store when the safe was opened and contents rifled through, personally emphasized to us the need of a local police force to govern the area.

Chapter 22

Retirement from the Hudson Bay Company

In 1950 I was finally pensioned off after serving some forty-five years for the Company and I must confess the thought of this had been worrying me considerably as I began to realize the implications. Having consoled myself during my lifetime job with the Company that whilst the salary was low, the fringe benefits in the shape of good living quarters and food for my family, made up for it.

Now however, I realized I would be starting from scratch with neither house nor furniture and mighty little money in the bank. Well, at least the Company was good enough to present me with a bonus of five hundred dollars, and my first move was to buy a small house from a closed down lumber camp near Geraldton and have it hauled on a flat bed to a lot that I had purchased from the Company.

Prior to the moving of the house I purchased some cedar posts from the Longlac Pulp and Paper Company and, with Tony's help, got them ready to set the house on. Believe me, it was a real hard task making the holes through the hard pan. In building a house on the ground, hardpan, sometimes referred to as ouklip, was a term used to describe a layer of soil usually found in the uppermost topsoil layer.

There were different types of hardpan but this one sure had fused and binded soil particles to create such a hard-working surface.

I was still living in the Company house and working, so my preparations for the foundations were confined to long evenings and slack periods. That summer Lorna, Jack and the family came up and paid me a visit and it was sure good to see them. I went fishing with Jack a couple of times, once at " 95" where he had a nice catch and another time to look into the Lake where the fish could be seen but not caught, at any rate, by any means we had at our disposal. Neither Jack nor I were accomplished fly fishermen and that was the only way they could be caught, so we returned home empty handed to find that Tony hadn't had much better success making holes for my foundation posts.

Not long after this, my house arrived and was duly deposited on the foundation we'd set up and I used all the time I could spare making alterations in the interior, building kitchen cupboards and installing a sink that would drain outside into an improvised septic tank. We had no well and when we subsequently moved in we had to avail ourselves of the nearby neighbors' well.

We hadn't moved into the house very long before Lisa suggested we should try and sell the place and move to Port Arthur, and I agreed, if I could get what I wanted for the place. Lisa had reminded me of all the hardships that would probably be involved when winter came.

Well, that was one time fortune smiled on me and I was able to get my price for the house, and not only that but was able to find an ideal spot in Port Arthur. I had slim hopes of being able to pay off the mortgage; but, thanks to Mildred's assistance and later on, Edith's, both of whom were working, I was able to do so. I did promise them a half interest in the property for their efforts. How very fortunate I was to have such helpful daughters who, in fact, between Tony and them, had bought all the furniture.

It was early in November 1950 that Lisa and I moved, Edith having decided to get a room at the Longlac Hotel and stay there, as she was employed as switch board operator by the Longlac Pulp & Paper Company. Tony was in Port Arthur and Ethel was spending her holidays with Shirley down at McTeir.

I had all our furniture, barring the stove, which I sold, transported by Lakehead Freightways Truck and I rode with the driver who had not had any sleep for forty-eight hours or so he said. He had a nap once in awhile for a few minutes en route, pulling to a stop and resting with his head on the steering wheel. My big concern was lest he'd doze off whilst driving, so I tried to engage him in conversation to keep him awake.

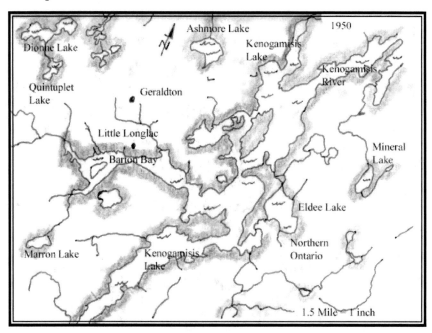

As it was, we developed some malfunction of the brakes; so, on arriving in Port Arthur, the driver was afraid to tackle the hill and parked overnight at Current River after first letting our two dogs, Patches and Fritz and me, off at our son George's house where Lisa was awaiting our arrival.

Perhaps I should digress here to say a few words about our dogs. Patches was a mongrel with a white haired terrier's characteristics, but was white with black patches, had extremely soulful eyes, especially when begging, could climb a ladder, loved the water and had a most tenacious grip with its teeth hanging onto an object at the end of a string while swinging around off its feet. Patches, I think, belonged to Tony, most dogs of ours being appropriated by him as his.

Fritz, however, a large dog with collie characteristics, but half as large again as the average collie, was Ethel's dog, having been given to her by Scotty Goulds, who was a friend of the family's. He was originally the property of a German prisoner of war. Huge as it was, it was harmless and loved to play with the kids. It did, however, come home one day with one of the neighbor's chickens, but Ethel was emphatic that Fritz must have been dead when the chicken was found. She just knew Fritz wouldn't kill it. I expect she had visions of my insisting that she would have to get rid of the dog.

Alas, we hadn't been in our new home more than a month or two when Fritz was found dead in a neighbor's yard, the owner of which was suspected of having poisoned it.

What an ideal spot the house was, situated on high ground from which, looking out my kitchen window, I could see the lake in the distance of some two miles away and Thunder Cape (Nanabijou), along with the top of Mount McKay from the front windows. To the west of us was a hill that unfortunately blocked out the sun an hour or two before it was due to set.

The back of the house was all nature undisturbed with small

groups of jack pine, spruce and poplar; there were also lots of willows and a high bluff of rocks from which one could view about two hundred and fifty degrees of a circle embracing the large vistas of Lake Superior, Mount McKay and the grain elevators on the waterfront.

There was also a small creek known as Vicke's Creek in which were brook trout, but with the exception of a small rainbow trout, I never caught anything worth keeping. Later, it was stocked annually with fingerlings and some larger ones just prior to the May twenty-fourth holiday, but as it was stated that the fishing was reserved for the children, I abandoned fishing in the creek in case my efforts to catch anything proved worthwhile.

It was in November that we moved into our new quarters and my first concern was the fact that the storm windows had not yet been put on. The window frames were already coated with heavy ice and it was debatable if and when they could be put on. Fortunately, a mild spell shortly after our arrival solved our first problem.

Our next problem was water, our well having gone dry during the winter, and so George came to the rescue by climbing down it and digging out some of the sand at the bottom.

Shortly after our arrival in Port Arthur, Ethel returned from McTier and took up residence with us, as well as Tony who had been working at odd jobs in the city, and whom I managed to get employment with the Department of Highways. In the early spring of 1951, Ethel got married to Philip Dorzak, whom she'd known at Longlac, and they rented a house of their own.

Chapter 23

Native Population Census & back to the HBC

I THINK IT was in the spring of 1951 that the Native agent Mr. Gerry Burke engaged me to accompany him on his treaty payment trip to take the census of the Native population at the various reserves which received treaty money. First, I think, we went to the nearest one which was at Squaw Bay back of Mount McKay near Fort William.

Squaw Bay reserve was a picturesque spot on the shores of Lake Superior. In the not too distant background could be seen Pie Island, which was probably named after those deep English pies. It had a Roman Catholic Church and a school.

Here I found the Natives all conversant with the English language so my knowledge of the Native language was superfluous. It was nice, however, to make the acquaintance of the Natives who were all strangers to me. One of the Natives, who had been in the army overseas, spun me a yarn which I hardly took to be original and this is how it went.

Some of his army buddies, on learning that he was a Native, made some comments about his not having any Native apparel, head feathers and other such stuff and asked him what his Native name meant. He said that it meant Running Water. He was then asked if he had any children to which he replied that he had two and that one was called Hot while the other Cold.

We then headed towards Pays Platte, Rossport, Heron Bay and Mobert. Pays Platte was a very small community. I was designated to proceed there solo and list the two or three families residing there, and the treaty party would pick me up en route to Rossport. Our stop at that reserve was brief.

At Heron Bay, to which I'd never been before, we found a fairly large number of Natives and amongst them an old man named Peter Moses, my midnight visitor of some twenty-two years ago at Longlac who, at that time, was wanted for murder. Just what the outcome was of what happened I didn't inquire and the old man seemed quite harmless and friendly so I didn't bring the matter up.

Our next stop was at Montezambert, now known as Mobert, and there I had the opportunity of briefly renewing my acquaintance with some of the Natives I had come in contact with during my brief spell of relieving the Post Manager some forty years or more previously. This reserve was not a picturesque spot, being situated as it was on a hillside near the Canadian Pacific Railway. At least I found the Hudson Bay Company had built a better store and was operating the post office.

Our next trip was to be around Lake Nipigon but first we returned to Port Arthur. A few days later we took off for Lake Nipigon, where we embarked at Brunt Bay. The weather was fine and first call was at Gull Bay, where I noted some improvement in the housing conditions. Here again, I met some of the Natives I'd known back in 1910. Passing up the west shore in our motor launch, the site of the old Nipigon House Post was hard to distinguish, having long since been closed and the site overgrown with poplar and willows.

What a pity such a picturesque spot should have to be abandoned as presumably all the Natives had moved to Gull Bay and none of their former habitations were in evidence.

Our next stop was at Wabinoosh Bay where we did some angling for pickerel which we caught in abundance. We then proceeded along the north shore of Lake Nipigon until we came to Mud River where we also enjoyed some good pickerel fishing and spent the night at a tourist camp there.

The next day we followed the east shore back to Brunt Bay and as there was a strong south-westerly wind and very little shelter in the way of islands, we were exposed to the full fury of the wind blowing across some fifty miles of lake. Some of our passengers became seasick but, surprisingly, I was not. At Brunt Bay, we stayed long enough to buy some ice with which to keep our fish fresh until we got home.

There was a church at Nakina, and I was surprised to learn that the large stained glass window behind the altar had been donated by a Native from Fort Hope by the name of John Yesno, in memory of his deceased wife, and I believe a son of this same man became a television actor in the seventies.

We went back to Port Arthur. I managed to keep myself occupied getting ready for the winter by saving up some huge logs from some old docks. I think they were anyway as they were all pretty well waterlogged. All I had was a two man cross-cut saw and an "Armstrong" engine; I found the manipulation of the two-man saw not very satisfactory. When Tony was home he gave me a hand with this task as well as digging up the sod in front of the house and removing the twitch grass, preparatory to making a lawn. Some of this ground we planted with potatoes, but the crop was so poor; half of what we planted had gone to waste We decided to try elsewhere the next year.

Came Christmas Eve and Ethel had her first daughter Margaret, but who was to become known as Nikki, and which she much preferred. I rather think it was Mildred who gave her that name and she was quite an adorable child.

In the fall of 1952, I think it was, I decided to put in a lawn and a carragana hedge along the front of our property, and plough up or rather dig up a potato patch on one of our spare lots.

It was then that I received a long distance phone call from the Hudson Bay Company in Winnipeg, Manitoba, asking if I'd care to act as relief manager at their post at the north-west end of Thunder Lake, the post being known as Brochet having, I believe, been moved from its original site on Lac du Brochet, a smaller lake to the north.

After accepting the job without just realizing exactly where the post was, I went down town and located the place on a large wall map in the CNR station. I then had serious qualms about how I'd manage in such an isolated spot among the Natives, who would undoubtedly speak a different language that the Ojibwas.

It was therefore a matter of considerable relief to learn on my arrival in Winnipeg that there was an Army Signal station there as well as a Roman Catholic Mission and, in fact, a fair number of English-speaking people.

My journey took me by train to Prince Albert, Saskatchewan and thence by plane to Lac La Ronge, Saskatchewan, stopping off at Isle La Crosse to land a few passengers amongst whom were a couple of Roman Catholic Nuns.

This was my first trip on a plane, barring a five or ten minute spin on one with Ethel at an outdoor celebration near Geraldton. I must confess that being cooped up in a cabin in which we sat sideways on some freight and without being able to see outside was not my idea of a joy ride by any means; but, on arriving at Lac La Ronge and finding I'd be taking a "Norseman" in from there and that I'd be the only passenger, I was able to sit beside the pilot, and I enjoyed the scenery from then on flying through the clouds.

The landing at Brochet Post involved quite steep banking but having viewed such operations many times, I was prepared for it. I found the spot quite attractive and the manager and his wife were glad to see me, after having been unable to get out for a holiday for some three years, I believe. There was very limited time for instructions from them as they were scheduled to leave the next day by the same plane.

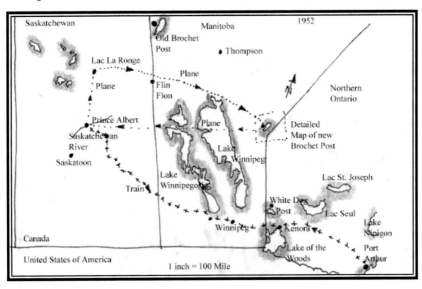

Mrs. Garbutt, the manager's wife, had very considerately baked up a quantity of bread which she'd sent over to the signal station to keep in their deep freeze and from which I could get as required.

I was next made acquainted with a Métis by the name of Henry Linklater who was the assistant in the store and who could interpret the Chippewayan language for me. It was not long after the Garbutts left that I was visited by a Hudson Bay Company Inspector in connection with the purchase of some stock that was being taken over from an opposition free trader who was going out of business.

During his stay, I received word of the death of my son-in-law Philip (Ethel's husband) in an elevator explosion atop Pool #4 elevator at Port Arthur. This was of course very upsetting, but, since my son George was there to look after his sister's welfare, I expressed my willingness to remain at the post for the duration of the job.

My next arrival was a large Canso Aircraft piloted by a Mr. Bamb, who, I believe, was flying some Native children back to their homes after the school they'd been attending had burnt down. After all the Natives had left for their trapping grounds, and the weather was suitable, I'd go for walks in the bush and noted quite a lot of caribou horns laying bleached among the moss, and low bush cranberries, and I was told that it was quite a common sight to see the caribou from the post during their migrations. We were only some thirty miles or so south of the barren lands, I was told.

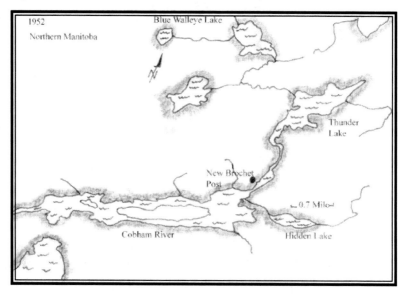

I struck up an acquaintance with an elderly man named Christian who had some very interesting stories to tell me, he having lived there a long time and who was in fact married to a Native of Chippewayan extraction, I believe, and who was taken ill and had to be flown to a hospital.

I hadn't been at the post long before I was promised a clerk by the Inspector. He arrived shortly after his departure. I have forgotten the clerk's name but not the quality of his services which weren't up to what I'd been used to expect, but probably up to current day standards.

It must have been in October that Mr. and Mrs. Garbutt returned to the post and I was to fly out the following day, and had been worrying that I might well be stuck there over the freeze up. As it was, the following morning the plane was all covered with frozen snow and sleet and we were consequently delayed in our take-off until around noon when it thawed sufficiently for us to do so.

We were advised at the last minute that we were to land at some barren point en route out to pick up some ailing Native woman, but we ran into a snowstorm and, whilst we made an effort to locate the place on which there was supposed to be a shack, we were unable to find it and the pilot stated he could not delay any longer. After calling in at the south end store to pick up the outgoing mail, we arrived at Lac La Ronge just in time for me to catch the last plane out for Prince Albert. It was a standard flight, but the only people flying were airplane company employees going out for the winter. I had to fly at my own risk.

This plane turned out to be an Otter aircraft and we landed in the Saskatchewan River, around dusk, nearly dark in fact. We then all piled into a small motor launch, nearly upsetting it, and someone jokingly remarked that the plane trip had perhaps been the least hazardous.

As the train had a long stop at Saskatoon, I found time to visit the Bay Store there and buy myself a badly needed overcoat.

Chapter 24

Two pensions and another retirement

When I arrived home after a day's stopover in Winnipeg, I found our daughter Ethel and her baby had come to live with us following the loss of her husband. The following January she gave birth to a second daughter Phyllis, named after her father Philip. We became quite a full house and it was well that I was able to convert a shed into a summer cottage utilizing some of Ethel's furniture after first re-flooring it and papering the walls and ceiling.

Fortunately the Saskatchewan Elevator Co. made a small settlement for herself and the children which enabled them to get by. Prior to getting the shed made habitable we borrowed a large tent about twelve feet by sixteen feet which we made good use of during the summer.

Alas in 1957 Ethel became involved in a bad car accident, being thrown some distance from the car, and she received some broken ribs and head injuries from which she never fully recovered. Her two young daughters were sent to Longlac where Edith became their guardian, or foster mother.

And so the years slipped by with little of interest, but during which I was able to obtain a part time job in the receiving room of a department store in Fort William and which I hung on to until

I was seventy years of age, when the store changed hands. As I was now receiving two pensions, one from the Bay and my old age security, I decided I should retire and not be looking for other jobs when there was so much unemployment around the country.

I must say, however, that retirement was not all I anticipated it would be. There was not always something to do. When I was young, in the spring and summer there was always something to do outside, what with the garden and sundry repairs and painting jobs.

Fortunately, at this time, George decided to get rid of his raspberry canes and so I made a new raspberry patch which proved to be quite fruitful, yielding us about forty quarts or so a year from which I made jam, jelly and preserves.

George also gave me a cluster of dahlia roots which he could do without. The dahlia was used as food and for decorative and medicinal purposes along with other uses such as making pipes from its tuberous stems. To me, they were just really nice flowering plants which made my home attractive looking. In fact, soon I had so many I couldn't even give them away. The new tubers were as prolific as the spuds and just seemed to thrive in that sandy soil. I also planted a hedge of carragana which from small four inch plants rapidly grew into a full hedge in the space of two years.

We didn't have a roller for the lawn. We made one from pouring concrete inside a metal drum into which a round iron rod was incorporated in the centre, leaving the two ends projecting and over which the looped ends of a rope could be slipped. It was a pretty heavy roller, and it worked, so well, in fact, that a neighbor borrowed it and neglected to return it.

The bane of our gardening activities was twitch grass, otherwise known as "crab grass", which seemed impossible to get rid of. We were told it had been actually planted there originally to keep the sand from blowing around. For quite a number of years, the blowing sand from the vacant bare ground was quite a nuisance and helped one realize what a sandstorm in the Sahara must have been like.

We had neither sewer nor city water connection, and were dependent on an outside well for our water supply; and, for the first year or two, we used it to keep our perishables, such as butter and milk cool as we had no fridge. There was also a standpipe across the street from which we could procure water when our well went dry. It must have been some three years before we were finally able to persuade the city authorities to give us water and sewer connections.

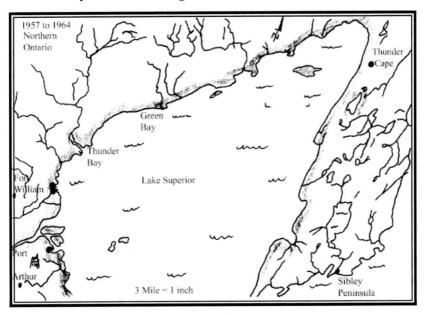

In these earlier years of our stay here, there were numerous paths through the jack pines and willows, and wild raspberries and blueberries were to be had about a half mile or so from the house.

Our rather humdrum existence was however brightened by the occasional visit of Edith and Mac, whom she had married in 1953 and the wedding took place in Longlac. Mildred also occasionally paid Lisa and me a visit whilst residing in Geraldton. Lorna, Jack and their three youngsters also paid us various visits.

Mildred got married in Toronto in 1955. I was the only one from home attending the wedding, but Edith and Mac were there as were Lorna, Jack and their youngest son. After the wedding I accompanied Lorna back to their home in Keene, New Hampshire, going by way of Gananoque, Ontario through Watertown in the United States and the Adirondack Mountains, which was a mountain range in the north-eastern part of New York State. After passing through the mountain range, which I enjoyed, we headed through the State of Vermont, passing Fort Ticonderoga en route.

Fort Ticonderoga was a large eighteenth century fort built at the narrows near the south end of Lake Champlain in upstate New York, and had been constructed by the French between 1754 to 1757 during the Seven Years' War which was sometimes called the French and Indian War in the USA. It was also used, but to a lesser extent, during the American Revolutionary War.

At one spot, where we stopped for lunch, Robert, who couldn't have been more than two years old, threw his mother's glasses out of the car window, unknown to us until we had gone a half mile or so. On discovering they were missing, we returned to where we'd parked the car and, sure enough, there they were, on the ground, and how fortunate for us as they were unbroken. Lorna said she could not have driven long without them.

What a memorable trip that was, traveling through new scenery, stopping off at one place to visit a small zoo that turned out to be a mink farm with a few bears, llamas and foxes.

From Fort Ticonderoga, we followed Route 22 to White Hall which was an historic home located in the state of Maryland. It consisted of three sections, the east wing, center wing and the west wing.

I read that part of the home had been destroyed in a fire in 1890 and then rebuilt in 1900. The house had been passed on from family to family for well over one hundred years, cared for and owned by the Ligon and Hains families which had joined together in 1930 by a marriage.

We crossed into the state of Vermont, thence onto Route 4 to Rutland, thence south south-east to Keene. This was my first visit there and how I loved that spot where Lorna and Jack had their house, close to a pond and surrounded by large pines and hemlocks, an ideal spot to my way of thinking. I was also able to see quite a lot of New Hampshire and Vermont accompanying Jack on many of his business trips.

One day, Lorna drove me and her youngsters to Hampton beach, a beach resort within the town of Hampton in the state of New Hampshire. There, we spent a delightful day and picnicked on the shores of the Atlantic. It was the first time I'd seen it since I'd come to Canada. My enthusiasm even led to my rolling up my trousers and going for a wade, and what a short one that was! I'd no idea the water could be so cold on a shallow sandy beach!

During my stay at Lorna and Jack's, the newlyweds, Mildred and Art, were honeymooning through the states visiting an uncle of ours in Stanford, Connecticut, and they picked me up en route. We returned by way of Albany through the New York throughway to Buffalo and thence via Niagara Falls. There, we stopped for an hour or so to view one of nature's most beautiful sites. Then, we continued towards Toronto where I saw Art and Mildred's home. Then, it was a long train ride home for me.

Mildred and Art then moved to Barrie. I visited them there in 1956. I liked where they were staying, the house being situated on Peel Street which had trees on both sides, whose branches overlapped at the top. They were then building a home of their own on the outskirts of what was then Allandale but is now part of Barrie.

I was able to give Art a hand painting the outside of the house and putting up the eaves troughs.

Well, the scenery was much to be desired compared to that around Lorna's, but at least they had lots of property and lost no time in putting some of it under cultivation, more in fact than they could actually look after.

En route home, I stopped off at Longlac to see how Edith and Mac were making out in the house they recently bought, and I was quite amazed to note the growth of the town since I'd left it last time.

In 1962, Ethel passed away following a brief illness in the hospital although she had been ailing for a long time, although not incapacitated. Her daughters arrived with Edith from Longlac and were able to see her for a few brief minutes around noon at which time it was not anticipated her end was so near. I received a call from the hospital late in the evening and George drove me there but, alas she had already passed away before we arrived.

Two years later, on May 13th my wife Lisa followed her, never regaining consciousness following a major operation, from which, had she recovered, she would have wished she hadn't, so perhaps it was all for the best.

In 1964, there were just Tony and me left to fend for ourselves, but that was no problem as I'd taken over a lot, if not all, of the household chores for some time as Lisa was an invalid for a number of years prior to her death.

In the following spring, I joined the Senior Citizens Friendship Club and, a year later, was appointed as Treasurer. At that time, we met every Friday afternoon in the hall of Dawson Court's home for the aged. I also joined the Port Arthur Pensioners, as well as the Sunshine Club and the Golden Age Club of Fort William. The following year, however, I decided two clubs were enough and so I dropped the Pensioners and Sunshine Clubs.

I cannot honestly say that I got much enjoyment from the meetings of our Senior Citizens Friendship Club. We badly needed to replace our president of sixteen years, but nobody had the heart to vote against her. Poor old soul! She was trying so hard to make a go of it, but it was too much for her.

For me the only attractions were the summer picnics, the bus rides and the occasional banquet at Thanksgiving and Christmas.

Bus trips to so called picnics were usually to Kakabeka Falls, where the picnic consisted of a good turkey dinner put up either by the Legion or some Church Women's group, followed by a visit to the falls where we'd have a few outdoor games in the park if weather permitted.

Kakabeka Falls was a waterfall on the Kaministiquia River located beside the village of Kakabeka Falls; it was around nineteen miles from the Thunder Bay area. The falls dropped one hundred and thirty-one feet, cascading into a gorge carved out of the Precambrian shield by melted water following the last glacial movement. With its size and ease of access, it had been nicknamed "the Niagara of the North".

What a big disappointment one bus trip turned out to be! It was a wet day and we were all forced to sit in the bus which was parked in the parking lot and just spend the afternoon waiting to leave. Supper that time was to be in the church basement and we were not welcome there until preparations were done. This we found hard, as many of us were in our seventies and eighties.

At such times as we had the Legion cater our supper, though, their ample hall was available to us before the meal and the piano could be played to accompany those who enjoyed singing. As well, we could use the hall for dances in which many engaged, including some octogenarians.

Chapter 25

A visit home to England

In 1966, Art and Mildred planned a trip to England to visit Art's aunt and uncle. They asked me if I would like to come with them to England since I hadn't visited it since I ran away at the age of fifteen. I decided I should go along because I especially wanted to visit my sister Flo whom I hadn't seen since 1902. The thought of traveling and seeing England where I was born permitted me one more time to quench my wanderlust.

Leaving Toronto airport around nine p.m. and stopping in Montréal, Québec to pick up additional passengers, we arrived at Heathrow Airport in London, England around eleven p.m. after a flight of around six hours, much of which was spent viewing the clouds below and the mountain peaks of Greenland. We had a very pleasant passage with a minimum of turbulence.

Rather a strange thing happened as we were leaving the airport, when I was approached by some gentleman saying that he believed he knew me. Well, I certainly didn't recognize him, and was full of suspicion until he mentioned his name and how he used to know me away back in 1927 when he was working for the forestry at Longlac, Ontario. Truly this was a small world after all.

We next proceeded to Victoria Station in England where I parted from Mildred and Art, who left for Liverpool Street Station from whence they were to entrain for Clacton in Essex. I caught a taxi to Paddington whence I'd catch a train to Taunton where my sister Flo was living.

Having an hour or more to wait for the train, I felt the need to go to the washroom downstairs to clean up. I wasn't much impressed with the way I felt after the long flight and I foolishly took off my coat and hung it on a coat rack well in sight of a mirror. Whilst in the midst of shaving I noticed a shady looking character enter by a different door, who brushed past my coat walking very busily. When I was through with my ablutions and put on my coat, I was distressed to find a book of train travel tickets missing, which I'd foolishly left in my breast pocket. I'd had little sleep on the plane during the six hour flight, much of which was taken up with a two a.m. meal, and gazing out the window until it became light.

Consequently, I was pretty well tuckered out but consoled myself with thoughts of the good nap I'd have on the express train. Alas, I'd just nicely started to doze off when another train whizzed past us from the other direction. It made such a noise I nearly jumped out of my seat, much to the amusement of my fellow passengers. The express trains sure do travel over there and went speeding so fast that I couldn't read the names of the stations although they were largely displayed.

It must have been around four p.m. when I arrived at Taunton, a town in Somerset County. There weren't many passengers around and I had no trouble finding my sister Flo who, no doubt, had decided to wear the apparel she'd had on in a recent colored snapshot that she'd sent me.

What a greeting that was after all these years!

I spent two weeks with my sister Flo. Mildred and Art came

down and met her and they stayed nearby. We visited Cheddar, a large village and civil parish in the District of Sedgemoor which was also in the County of Somerset. It gave its name to cheddar cheese and was a major centre for strawberry picking.

There, we saw Cheddar Gorge which was the largest in the United Kingdom and several show caves. We looked at the gorge, where supposedly the hymn "Rock of Ages" had been composed by the author who was sheltering under some large overhanging rock. "Rock of Ages" was a popular Christian Hymn by Reverend Augustus Montague Toplady. It was written in 1763 and then published in "The Gospel Magazine" in 1775.

According to a famous but largely unsubstantiated story, Reverend Toplady drew his inspiration from an incident in the gorge. He was a preacher in a nearby village of Blagdon. He was traveling along the gorge when he was caught in a storm. Finding shelter in a gap, he was suddenly struck by the title and scribbled the initial lyrics on a playing card.

Our limited time prevented us from taking a trip up the gorge. We did all our sightseeing by Double Decker buses, always riding upstairs so we could see over the hedges. These were often so high as to block the view for those seated below.

How wonderful it was to renew my acquaintance, after all these years, with the scenes of the many small villages, all with their beautiful churches with their massive towers or steeples!

We were rather amused on one trip when some fellow passenger voiced her criticism of having to pay for the dog she was carrying and the fact that it was denied a seat. We told her that, in Canada, dogs weren't even allowed on the buses to which she replied "Oh, I thought everybody in Canada did what they pleased."

On another occasion, some friends of Flo took us out for a drive.

They let me off to admire some thatched cottage and its lovely garden. The owner came out to talk and, on learning that I was from Canada, told me that he used to work for the Canadian Pacific Railway, somewhere out west. We had an interesting talk and then I explored around the area for a while.

We also made a trip to Dunster Castle which was most interesting. The castle was the historical home of the Luttrell family located in the small town of Dunster, Somerset. There had been a castle at the top of the hill at Dunster for more than one thousand years and it was granted by William the Conqueror to William de Mohum whose family lived there until the castle was sold in 1376 by Lady Joan de Mohum to Lady Elizabeth Luttrell. Her descendants still owned the castle while we were visiting it.

The castle dominated a steep hill overlooking the picturesque village of Dunster, and had been fortified since Saxon times, although nothing remained of these early defenses. I had heard that, during the early medieval period, the sea reached the base of the hill offering a natural defense and that it also had strong walls, towers, ramparts and outworks which protected the other sides.

All that remained now of the medieval fortifications were the impressive gatehouse and the stumps of the two towers. The castle was modified and changed over the centuries and much of the current appearance dated from the 18th century when the park was landscaped and the Green court and the terraced grounds were created.

For the last two weeks, I had visited Taunton and the surrounding countryside in Somerset County. During the next week, though, I was going to visit London and the towns of the scenes of my boyhood days. How I longed to see Clacton, Colchester, Lexdon, Ipswich, Harwich, Mistley and Manningtree! Would they be much changed?

First, we went to Clacton where we were the guests of Art's uncle. I found English geography different after living in Canada so long and couldn't remember if it was Great Clacton which was a locality in the Tendring district of Essex County. There was also Clacton-on-Sea and to the north and south-east was the village of Little Clacton.

I found Clacton quite strange, but then I had only been there on one or two occasions some sixty odd years ago. Unlike Somerset, which had come through the war unscathed, Essex County was part of what was known as Hells Corner during the war, I believe.

During my stay at Taunton, Art and Mildred had spent a week or so on daily visits to London, so we only made one trip there, during which we visited St. Paul's Cathedral which Mildred was anxious to see. There, we took part in a short service that was in progress whilst other disinterested tourists were at liberty to wander around gazing at the various memorial tablets and other items.

Visiting St. Paul's Cathedral was very special to me, even with the annoyance of tourists wandering around during the mass.

On the plaque outside the cathedral was written that this was an Anglican Cathedral on Ludgate Hill in the city of London and it was the seat of the Bishop of London. The building we were looking at dated back to the 17th century and was generally thought to be London's fifth St. Paul's Cathedral. This was not counting every major medieval reconstruction as a new cathedral. It sat on the highest point of the City of London, which originated as the Roman trading post of Londinium situated on the River Thames.

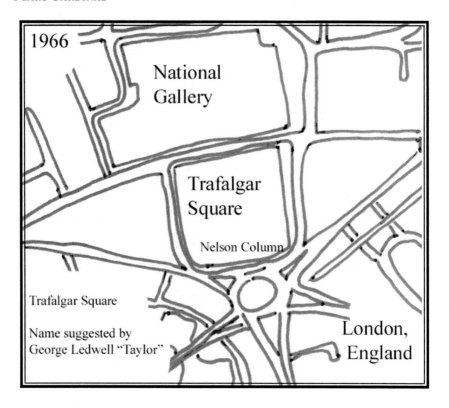

After our visit at the famous cathedral, we decided to go to Trafalgar Square. There, we spent some time with the pigeons which were so tame they'd alight on our shoulders. We observed some gentleman with his coat decorated with some of their droppings. I tapped him on the shoulder and called his attention to it, which Mildred thought I shouldn't have done , but I assured her that I'd much prefer such decorations be called to my attention than not.

Trafalgar Square was a square in central London England. With its unique position in the heart of London, it was one of the most famous squares in the United Kingdom and the world. We looked at the centre where Nelson's Column was guarded by four lion statues at its base. The name of the square was to commemorate the Battle of Trafalgar in 1805. This was a British naval victory during the Napoleonic Wars. Originally it was to be called "King William the Fourth Square" but George Ledwell Taylor suggested the name "Trafalgar Square".

I sat there wondering if he could be a relation of mine, having the last name Taylor. I had been born in 1887 and this chap George Taylor probably named this square before I was born.

We next caught a two Decker bus for the zoo, passing the comparatively new post office tower en route. The zoo was most interesting. At one point we lost Art, and Mildred and I took off for the aviary. There was quite a crowd assembled in front of a cage in which sat an American condor; but, it was rather a squirrel who had dashed into the cage and was squatting in the back corner that was attracting all the attention. The condor seemed to take no interest. Presently, a keeper came along and suggested that the crowd move back to let the squirrel exit the same way as it had entered. Failing this, the keeper entered the cage where the squirrel dashed into the adjoining cage occupied by an American Eagle, which promptly flew down from its perch and made short work of the squirrel, much to Mildred's distress, although I pointed out that such things were going on daily in their natural habitat.

I was a little worried about losing contact with Art, but Mildred didn't seem to be and we eventually met up with him when it was time to leave. He was able to explain to us all that we had missed about the history of one of the most famous zoos in the world, as he excitedly told us. London Zoo, he said, was the world's oldest scientific zoo. It was opened in London on April 27, 1828 and had been originally intended to be used as a collection for scientific study. Later it opened to the public in 1847.

Art told us that it roughly held around seven hundred and fifty-five species of animals. As well as being the first scientific zoo, London Zoo opened the first reptile house in 1849, the first public aquarium in 1853, the first insect house in 1881 and finally it opened the first children's zoo in 1938.

On Sunday, we attended morning services at which Mildred appeared to be the youngest one present. The church was small, but amply big enough for the congregation. The gardens roundabouts were beautiful with an abundance of roses.

Every morning we were awakened early by doves which seemed quite common in the vicinity; to me, doves and pigeons looked the same. Afterwards, I heard a knock on the bedroom door, announcing the arrival of our charitable hostess who was bringing up a cup of tea and a cookie as a wake up treat.

As I recollect, our next trip was to Colchester where we visited the old Roman Castle which was now a museum; it had been renovated to such an extent that it was unrecognizable to me as being the same one I'd visited in my boyhood. I couldn't remember the name of the castle but it could have been Rayleigh Castle, which was a masonry and timber one built near the town of Rayleigh in Essex County, England in the 11th century after the Norman Conquest.

Art just loved museums and we had invited his aunt and uncle to accompany us. After lunch, Art and his uncle decided to return to the castle whilst Mildred and Art's aunt went window shopping.

I caught a bus out to Lexden some two miles away to see if the old Quaker school was still there. Formerly a village, Lexden was now a suburb. It had been previously called Lessendon, Lassendene and Laexadyne.

The small village of Lexden had grown a lot, but the heart of the village remained unchanged and there was the old school house converted into an apartment house, but alongside were two big driveway gates through which I entered with some trepidation. I found the old classroom in complete disarray and the student desks removed and piled in what was formerly a stable for the principal's horses. There was the playground all covered with long grass and weeds, the scene of my first fight.

I took a short walk up a nearby hill to the scene of a small candy store, which was still there much as I remember it; we used to spend our pennies there and in those days a farthing (1/4 of a penny) could purchase a mouthful of sweets. My time however was too limited to spend as much time as I'd have liked looking around and so I caught the next bus back to Colchester and located the others at the castle.

Our next trip was to the outskirts of Ipswich. There, we had no specific points of interest to visit. We decided to visit the arboretum, which was a collection of trees. In reading a plaque, I noticed that a fruticetum meant fruit bearing plants and that a viticetum was a collection of vines. I picked up a couple of horse chestnuts as souvenirs of my visit to that park where I used to play as a child.

Mildred was quite intrigued with the stores and arcades and Art bought himself a heavy sweater at a very substantial saving over Canadian prices.

Of more interest to me now, however, was our next trip which would bring us to the port of Harwich where some of my renowned ancestors had been buried.

Harwich was another town in Essex, England and one of the Havenports, located on the coast with the North Sea to the east. The Havenports was a group of five ports on the east coast of England; traditionally, it consisted of three deep-water ports being those of Felixstowe, Ipswich and Harwich.

Instead of looking in the church where the secondary tablets commemorating their memory are still to be seen, I'd foolishly looked in the graveyard from which the ancient head stones had been removed. I'm sure this was such a disappointment for sister Flo, who had been so anxious for me to see them.

We then followed a seawall around past Landguard Fort which was on the River Orwell. It was designed to guard the entrance to Harwich. We went to the end of the seawall, and standing in the sand covered by tide-water, were the same old trees that had been there some sixty odd years ago, just one or two of the trees of which I remembered.

We next followed a street called Orwell Tivrace where I tried to identify the house where I went to school, but all the houses were identical and I could not be positive as to the correct one. Art decided to take my picture there anyway, but the photo failed to turn out.

We then found it was time for lunch and discovered to our dismay that all the restaurants were closed that afternoon. It was with a sigh of relief, however, that we finally located one near the Railroad Depot that was open and, it being a case of Hobson's choice, we settled for that.

Hobson's choice is a free choice in which only one option is offered, and one may refuse to take that option. The choice therefore was between taking the option or not; it was a "take it or leave it" option. I knew that this phrase was said to originate with Thomas Hobson who lived during the years of 1541 to 1631. He was a livery stable owner in Cambridge, England. To rotate the use of his horses, he offered customers the choice of either taking the horse in the stall nearest the door or taking none at all.

We then visited Mistley some ten miles away which we covered by bus. I found the core of the village practically unchanged, but noticed that the garden across the street from my granddad's house was all enclosed by a board fence over which we couldn't see, instead of a picket fence from long ago. The ornamental railing encircling the flower bed was also gone, having been commandeered during the First World War to help make ammunition for the defense of the country.

After viewing the property from the outside, we then followed a backcountry lane to the church, some half mile or so distant, whilst I was wondering if I'd have any difficulty locating my granddad's gravestone; there it was, right near the path we were following. It was amazing! Mildred and I entered the church and, after showing her the pew we used to occupy, I signed the visitor's book.

Afterwards we followed the main road back to Mistley House and Mildred and I summoned up our courage to knock on the front door and announce to the young lad who opened it that I had lived here a long time ago. He excused himself and brought his father to the door, who was most kind and co-operative. He first apologized for the state of the house into which they had only recently moved and were in the process of getting settled. Then, he started taking us through the entire house where I noticed great changes had been made; at least, my bedroom was just the same except that it was adorned with numerous horses racing on wall posters.

We were then shown through the garden which was nothing like it used to be, the large conservatory having been demolished as well as the fernery, and the stable with its tile floor was in badly neglected condition. No doubt it had not been used since granddad's time. Following the tour around we were invited in for tea and sandwiches, and on learning that we were going to Manningtree, our hostess said she was driving there in her car which was a Jaguar and she would be glad to drive us over. On the way, I caught a glimpse of some five hundred or so swans that were raised in the vicinity near the two towers of the old historic church.

I neglected to mention the Maltings in Mistley; these were in my boyhood days quite imposing structures. A malt house or malting was a building where cereal grain was converted into malt by soaking it in water, allowing it to sprout and then drying it to stop further growth. The malt was used in brewing beer and making whisky. It was also added to certain foods.

We entered one of the abandoned buildings and, in one room, we found what looked like some mechanical contraption for weighing and bagging. The building and its contents really intrigued me.

We saw ships from European ports, largely Scandinavian, with their crews of foreigners. Mistley and Manningtree were actually on the estuary of the river Scour, which at this point attained a width some eight or ten miles distant. Come low tide though it was just a small narrow stream a few yards' width. Through the mud, along the banks of the narrow stream, we enjoyed ourselves observing herons.

Getting back to our visit to Manningtree, however, we got out of the car at the beginning of the main street where I was able to show Mildred the house that we had occupied back in 1891. This street didn't appear to have changed at all, and there stood the same shoe store operating under the same name that it did when I used to go there to be fitted for shoes. Having shopped around in Taunton and elsewhere for a pair of comfortable, but rather out of style shoes, I suggested to Mildred that I would try out this store, and there in short order discovered what turned out to be the most comfortable shoes that I have had in years, and for which six years later, I've continued to wear after having resoled them twice.

We visited a small novelty shop where Mildred bought a few souvenirs. Then I took her down to the old sawmill that was still operating under the name Taylor and Butler, although my grandfather had been dead close to seventy years. We also visited the old flour mill, which I remembered as the scene of the Constables' famous paintings.

We then walked around one of the side streets before catching our bus back to Holland-on-Sea, which is a seaside town in East Essex. It was located south of the little village of Great Holland and directly north of Clacton-on-Sea. From there it was just a short coastal walk down the coastline to Clacton.

When we arrived, Art's aunt had a delicious repast made for us, including the delicious dessert known as trifle which was made with Devonshire cream amongst other ingredients. It was simply out of this world!

During our three week stay in England there had been practically no rain but lots of heavy fog in the mornings that didn't clear until around noon, but the day we left for Canada it was pouring rain. As I sat in the busy Heathrow Airport, in London, England I thought back to the past and it seemed that at that moment my life had just gone full circle and that I was exactly where I had been when I ran away from home those sixty plus odd years ago as a youth of fifteen years of age. Now I was seventy-seven years old and I was happy to once more have had the chance to pursue my wanderlust and travel the countryside of England where I had been born.

I wondered if I had made the right choice in running away from home. Should I have remained in England living with my strict old granddad at a job which bored me? No, I decided. I had made the right choice in moving to Canada. I had experienced life like no other in my many wanderings and I hoped in my heart that I had made a difference in the life of the people that I had met in Canada. I thanked God for my wonderful family that he had given me.

Afterword

The journal continues on until Sydney Taylor was eighty years old.

While interesting, I thought it most appropriate that the story start in England and that it should end some sixty odd years later back there when he is re-united with his sister from his youth. To me, although he did a great many things after arriving back to Canada to what is present day Thunder Bay with the amalgamation of Port Arthur and Fort William, his story had gone full-circle and I wanted to end it with him sitting in Heathrow Airport in London, England.

Sydney Taylor died at the age of ninety-two in 1979 while living in Barrie, Ontario at his daughter's home and he was buried there.

From his journal, I gathered that Sydney Taylor seemed to have been a good Christian man. He often wrote about the various churches and seems to have helped everyone he came into contact with. He never complained or slacked off from his work in the places where he worked which was the rough outdoor existence of the early days of northern Ontario. If more people were like him, life would be easier and we would enjoy our lives, families and jobs a lot better.

Discussions and endless hours together between Walter Taylor

Jr. and his grandfather Sydney Taylor, whom the grandson knew very well and loved, makes me think that Walter Taylor Jr. learned a lot of his life skills from him.

Walter Taylor Jr. told me that Sydney Taylor started writing his journals in his early twenties. One of the family members took much time to decipher his finely scripted writing and typed it using an old fashioned typewriter before the days of the computer.

Now with the advent of the internet, people around the world can follow along on the travels of a Hudson Bay Company employee called Sydney Taylor and learn more deeply about every aspect of life that he encountered.

The journal has kept my wife Johanne and I fascinated and as you read it I hope you will feel the same.

Marc Cardinal

Brockville, Ontario

Biography

Since graduating from Cambrian College in Sudbury, Ontario with a Diploma in "Geological Engineering Technology" in 1984, my work background has tended to be split for the last twenty-six years between technical and sales work.

In technical job positions I've worked for many years in the wilds of northern Ontario, Saskatchewan and Québec searching for gold deposits.

I've also worked for various Government agencies like the Canadian Coast Guard, the Ministry of Agriculture, the Ministry of the Environment, the Ministry of Natural Resources, the Conservation Authorities, Engineering and Surveying firms to municipal technical jobs.

In sales I've had my own picture framing business for ten years starting from a home-based business to a large professionally equipped store. I've worked in grocery stores, galleries, camera stores, bookstores, restaurants.

Some people work their whole life at one job while others continually work at different jobs. In life there must be a reason for everything and maybe a mixed knowledge of people, places and things is what is required to be a successful writer.

Wanderlust

Marc Cardinal
Brockville, Ontario, Canada
silver_fox_73@hotmail.com

CPSIA information can be obtained at www.ICGtesting.com
Printed in the USA
LVOW11s1055020814